W9-CAD-185

This book is dedicated to the soldiers, sailors, airmen and civilians of the United States and Canada who for nearly four years fought not only an enemy but also physical hardship, loneliness and tedium in the great North Country of Canada and Alaska.

INTRODUCTION

In most combat theaters of the Second World War the combatants had to fight only each other. In Alaska and northwestern Canada, however, they also did battle with the weather, the wilderness and boredom. This remote territory was probably the war's least known and least publicized combat zone. Most of those who served there had never seen anything like it before, nor would they ever want to see it again.

Much of what happened in the North Country war was dictated by the whims of civilian and military leaders in Washington and Tokyo. On a global scale, it was an area of great importance for brief periods, but all but forgotten most of the time.

The United States fought World War II mainly in Europe, Africa and the islands of the southern and central Pacific. Yet it was in the Aleutians, in the northern Pacific that American territory was invaded. It was there that for the first time since the War of 1812, an enemy stood on U.S. soil.

Alaska and northwestern Canada were a gateway to the western coasts of both countries, and, conversely, to northern Japan and Siberia.

Largely because of its remoteness, the area had been neglected militarily for years. What some called "Seward's Folly" (after the secretary of state who negotiated the U.S. purchase of Alaska from Russia in 1867) was just that to most people involved in military planning.

The map makes clear the potential importance of the area in a war between the United States and Japan. People like Gen. Billy Mitchell, Anthony Dimond, Representative from Alaska, Gov. Ernest Gruening and Gen. S. B. Buckner tried to arouse military planners to its significance. They had little success, but once the area appeared to be threatened, a vast army of men and material descended on it. More than a billion dollars was spent on construction projects in the North Country.

In hindsight, one wonders whether this huge effort was necessary. But analysts and critics should put history in perspective. In late 1941 and early 1942 the Japanese were threatening American soil. The U.S. fleet was crippled after Pearl Harbor. War fever was sweeping the country.

I have tried to tell the story of the war through pictures, supplemented by enough text to provide an overall view. For a more detailed narrative of the war in the North, I recommend Brian Garfield's **The Thousand Mile War.** While reading books and articles on the subject, I was amazed by the number of inconsistencies and errors in dates, personalities and actions. Because of the secrecy that shrouded the fighting and construction work, discrepancies were inevitable. I have tried to present as accurate a record as possible.

Let us not forget the brave men and women who fought and died in this remote part of the world.

Stan Cohen
Missoula, Montana

To Pops 1995 from Scott & Michele Van Laer

Volume ONE

THE FORGOTTEN WAR

A PICTORIAL HISTORY OF WORLD WAR II
IN ALASKA AND NORTHWESTERN CANADA

To Pops 1995 from Scott & Michele Van Laer

Japanese naval airmen on Attu in 1942.   *USAF*

THE FORGOTTEN WAR

Volume ONE

A PICTORIAL HISTORY OF WORLD WAR II IN ALASKA AND NORTHWESTERN CANADA BY STAN COHEN

COPYRIGHT © 1981 BY STAN COHEN

All rights reserved. No part of this book may be used or reproduced without written permission of the publisher.

LIBRARY OF CONGRESS CATALOG CARD NO. 81-80570

ISBN 0-933126-13-1

First Printing: April 1981
Second Printing: October 1981
Third Printing: February 1982
Fourth Printing: January 1983
Fifth Printing: April 1983
Sixth Printing: July 1983
Seventh Printing: March 1984
Eighth Printing: May 1985
Ninth Printing: February 1986
Tenth Printing: October 1986
Eleventh Printing: May 1987
Twelfth Printing: January 1988
Thirteenth Printing: May 1989
Fourteenth Printing: December 1989
Fifteenth Printing: October 1990
Sixteenth Printing: October 1991
Seventeenth Printing: February 1993
Eighteenth Printing: March 1995

Printed in Canada
D. W. Friesen and Sons
Altona, Manitoba

Cover art work by Monte Dolack,
Missoula, Montana

Cover Photo — PBYs in Alaska:
Donald McKay
Little Rock, Arkansas

PICTORIAL HISTORIES PUBLISHING COMPANY
713 South 3rd West
Missoula, Montana 59801

ACKNOWLEDGEMENTS

A book of this scope could not have been written without the help of many persons in the United States and Canada. Dozens of men who served in the North Country in World War II wrote me or sent me photographs. Special thanks go to Lyman Woodman of Anchorage, who is writing his own Army history of Alaska and provided me with much information; Adm. James Russell of Tacoma, Wash., commander of VP-42 squadron in Alaska early in the war, who provided pictures and information and with his wife, opened his home to me; and Richard Finnie of Belvedere, Calif., the official historian of the Canol Project, who reviewed and corrected my chapter on Canol.

Many archives workers in the two countries were helpful. My thanks also to the following for information, pictures and encouragement:

My wife Anne and two children, John and Andy.
Bob McGiffert of Missoula for editing my manuscript.
Marlene Waylett of Missoula for technical assistance.
Don Miller of Missoula for much technical assistance.
Al Rogers, Allyn, Washington.
R. Adm. C. B. Jones, USN Ret., Coronado, California.
Lloyd Wickliff, Indianapolis, Indiana.
Russell Gettleman, Green Bay, Wisconsin.
Reuben Schiller, Rockford, Illinois.
Mrs. Jane Geitner Tucker, Old Tappan, New Jersey.
Mrs. Marilynn Hamlet, Seattle, Washington.
Clinton Dutcher, USN Ret., Inverness, Florida.
Frank Harvey, USA Ret., Haddon Heights, New Jersey.
Jack Haugen, San Leandro, California.
Thomas Pynn, St. Petersburg, Florida.
Robert Durkee, Helena, Montana.
Thomas Boardman, Boise, Idaho.
Craig Sorensen, Tacoma, Washington.
R. L. White, Cmdr. USN Ret., Lynn Haven, Florida.
Phylis Bowman, Prince Rupert, British Columbia.
Robert Oenbrink, Anchorage, Alaska.
Donald McKay, Little Rock, Arkansas.
Robert Olendorff, Anchorage, Alaska.
Kermit Edmonds, Missoula, Montana.
Dr. C. P. Brooke, Missoula, Montana
Gary Candelaria, Sitka, Alaska

PHOTO CREDITS

I have tried to select photographs that are representative of the many different aspects of the military campaign in Alaska and Canada. Although this war zone was not well known or publicized during the war or afterwards, it produced thousands of pictures from which to choose. Sources of photographs are identified by these abbreviations:

AAC	Alaskan Air Command - Elmendorf Air Force Base - Anchorage
AHL	Alaska Historical Library, Archives - Juneau
AHFAM	Anchorage Historical and Fine Arts Museum - Anchorage
BC	Boeing Company - Seattle
COE	Corps of Engineers, U.S. Army - Anchorage
DP	Dedman's Photo Shop - Skagway
FR	Fort Richardson, Public Relations Office - Anchorage
F&WS	U.S. Fish and Wildlife Service - Anchorage
GAI	Glenbow-Alberta Institute - Calgary
PAA	Provincial Archives of Alberta - Edmonton
RC	Adm. James Russell Collection - Tacoma
SC	Stan Cohen - Author's personal collection
UAA	University of Alaska Archives - Fairbanks
USA	U.S. Army Archives - Washington
USAF	U.S. Air Force Archives - Washington
USN	U.S. Navy Archives - Washington
UW	University of Washington - Seattle
YA	Yukon Archives - Whitehorse

Photos sent in by individuals are acknowledged by name and hometown.

TABLE OF CONTENTS

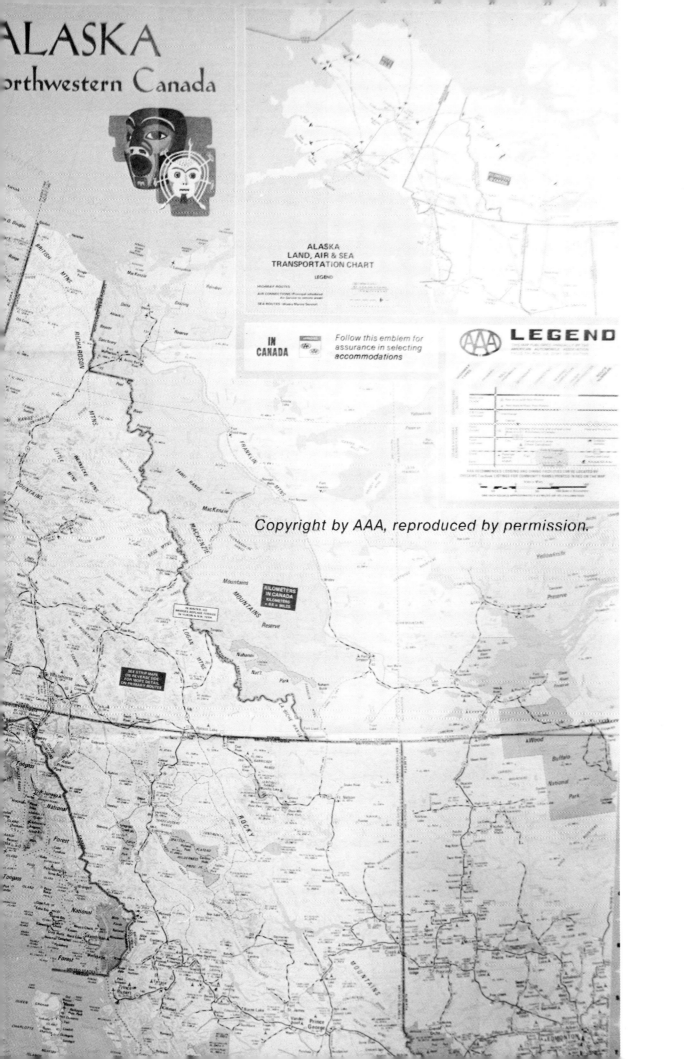

ALASKA
orthwestern Canada

ALASKA
LAND, AIR & SEA
TRANSPORTATION CHART

LEGEND

Follow this emblem for
assurance in selecting
accommodations

IN
CANADA

LEGEND

Copyright by AAA, reproduced by permission.

Fort William H. Seward near Haines, Alaska was built between 1902 and 1904. In 1922 its name was changed to Chilkoot Barracks. At the start of World War II it was the only military post in Alaska, housing 11 officers and 286 enlisted men. During the war it became an induction center and rest camp.

AHL

NORTH COUNTRY DEFENSES 1867-1941
SEWARD'S FOLLY TO PEARL HARBOR

The military policy of the United States in Alaska up to 1940 can be summed up in one word--neglect.

When the United States bought Alaska from Russia for $7.2 million in 1867, Sitka became the seat of government of the new possession and the site of the first military installation. Brevet Maj. Gen. Jefferson C. Davis (no relation to the President of the Confederate States of America) was appointed commanding general, Military District of Alaska, and served in the post until August 1870.

During the late 1800s and early 1900s, many forts were built in Alaska. Some of the more important were Forts Tongass and Wrangell in the southeast; Fort Kodiak on Kodiak Island; Fort St. Michael on Norton Sound; Fort Gibbon at Tanana; Fort Egbert at Eagle; Fort Liscum at Valdez; and Fort William H. Seward at Haines. Many other small posts were set up, several to provide law and order during the Klondike Gold Rush of 1897-99.

Other Army units were busy during these years conducting geographic and scientific expeditions and, in the early 1900s, setting up a communications system and road and trail networks.

The Army was in control of Alaska until 1877. Then the Treasury Department assumed responsibility, and in 1879 the Navy took over. Civilian government was established in 1884. Troops were withdrawn in 1877, but were sent back 20 years later during the Klondike Gold Rush.[1]

By 1910, most Army activity had been discontinued, not to be resumed on any large scale for 30 years. Fort William H. Seward at Haines was the only post still active.

During World War I, several units were stationed in Alaska primarily to guard the Alaska Railroad, but after the Armistice there was little interest in the defense of the Territory until World War II.

In 1904, the Navy designated Kiska Island in the Aleutians a naval reservation, but did not develop it. By the time the Navy looked at the island again, it was in the hands of the enemy.

In 1922, the United States, Japan and several other nations signed the Washington Conference Treaty limiting armaments. The United States agreed not to fortify the Aleutian Island chain, and the Navy scrapped a number of ships. All the Army posts in the Territory were closed except Fort William H. Seward, which was renamed Chilkoot Barracks. Japan renounced this treaty in 1934 without stirring any Amercan military response.

---

[1]Alaska officially became a United States Territory in 1912.

Gen. William "Billy" Mitchell, an outspoken critic of American indifference to military preparedness, told a Congressional hearing in 1935: "Alaska is the keystone of the Pacific arch. An aerial campaign against Japan can be pushed to best advantage from the territory.

"Japan is our dangerous enemy in the Pacific. They won't attack Panama. They will come right here to Alaska. Alaska is the most central place in the world for aircraft and that is true either of Europe, Asia or North America. I believe in the future, he who holds Alaska will hold the world, and I think it is the most important strategic place in the world."

Another proponent of Alaskan defense was Anthony Dimond, Alaska's delegate to the House of Representatives. He had pleaded with the House for years for money to build bases in Alaska. In

Brig. Gen. William "Billy" Mitchell, an aviator and early advocate of Alaskan Defense. He was first stationed in Alaska at Eagle working on the WAMCATS in 1902.   AAC

1934 he noted that use of Alaska could shorten the Great Circle Route between the United States and the Orient -- both for the United States and for an attacker.

But in the 1930s Congress was in no mood to appropriate funds for military construction, and it was not until 1940 that it approved $4 million for a "cold-weather testing station" for airplanes and material at Fairbanks.

The Navy, through a bill that became law on April 25, 1939, had proposed building air stations at Sitka and Kodiak, and these were under construction at the time of the attack on Pearl Harbor. The Navy also had a radio station at Dutch Harbor and maintained several radio direction-finder stations along the seacoast.

Onto this scene stepped a soldier with a famous

Lt. Gen. Simon Bolivar Buckner Jr. at his desk at Fort Richardson in June 1943. He was the commander of the Alaska Defense Command from July 1940 to June 1944, when he was transferred to the South Pacific. USA

namesake--Simon Bolivar Buckner Jr.[2] He was assigned to Alaska in July 1940 as commander of the newly-created Alaska Defense Force. He had a formidable job--to command a non-existent force.

Meanwhile, a rumor had started that Russia, in cooperation with Germany, had begun to build a military base on Big Diomede Island in the Bering Straits opposite Alaska.[3] Although it was false, the rumor impelled Congress to vote a record defense budget for Alaska. The rapid escalation of the war in Europe in 1940-41 and increasing Japanese activity in Asia caused Congress to appropriate money for air bases at Anchorage, Kodiak and Yakutat, a naval base at Dutch Harbor in the Aleutians and an airbase on Annette Island in southeastern Alaska.

The first new troops of the Alaska Defense Force -- 780 officers and men of the 4th Infantry Regiment, led by Lt. Col. Earl Landreth -- arrived at Anchorage on June 27, 1940, to supplement the troops at Chilkoot Barracks at Haines and a few hundred men of the Army Signal Corps scattered through the Territory. The new troops were the vanguard of nearly half a million who would eventually serve in Alaska and Canada.

In support of the military, the Civil Aeronautics Administration began building emergency landing fields with appropriations that totaled $48 million in 1940 and 1941. The first fields were built at Nome and Naknek, the latter on the Alaska Peninsula, providing access to the Aleutians. Other fields were at Galena, Northway, McGrath, Bethel, Big Delta and Gulkana. When war came these fields were improved by Army engineers and became important auxiliary air bases.

The "cold-weather testing station" at Fairbanks became Ladd Field,[4] and construction of the largest military establishment in Alaska began at Anchorage--Fort Richardson and Elmendorf Field.[5]

Territorial Gov. Ernest Gruening, who was appointed to his post in 1939,[6] was a strong ad-

---

[2]Buckner's father had been a famous general in the Confederate Army during the Civil War, governor of Kentucky from 1887 to 1891 and a candidate for vice president of the United States in 1896.

[3]Germany and Russia signed a non-aggression pact on Aug. 23, 1939. Russia was to remain neutral in case Germany went to war. This pact remained in effect until Germany's attack on Russia on June 22, 1941.

[4]Ladd Field was named for Major Arthur K. Ladd, who was killed in an air crash in South Carolina in 1935.

[5]Fort Richardson was named for Brig. Gen. Wilds P. Richardson, pioneer Alaska soldier, engineer and explorer. Elmendorf Field was named for Captain Hugh M. Elmendorf who was killed in a plane crash at Wright Field, Ohio in 1933.

vocate of Alaskan defense. He repeatedly petitioned the War Department for authority to organize an Alaska National Guard, and in mid-1940 the 297th Infantry Battalion was established. It was called to active service Sept. 15, 1941, and was sent to the United States for training. Several units did serve in Alaska during the war.

On Aug. 9, 1940, the first Air Corps personnel arrived at Merrill Field, Anchorage's municipal airport, in an old Martin B-10 bomber. Maj. Everett S. Davis became chief of aviation for the Alaska Defense Command and first commander of the 11th Army Air Force.

By the middle of 1941, Gen. Buckner was fighting an uphill battle to build Alaskan strengths for the war he knew was coming. Progress had been made, but defense of the Territory still depended on a tiny Air Force and a mere 8,000 troops spread thinly through southeastern Alaska, the interior and the Aleutians.

The bombs that fell on Pearl Harbor on Dec. 7, 1941, focused attention on the situation in Alaska. Hawaii had been bombed; would Alaska be next? Mitchell, Dimond and others had been warning of this possibility for years. But Alaska was not ready. It lay open to anything the Japanese planned for it.

The military strength in Alaska had expanded by Dec. 7 to approximately 22,000 Army troops, 2,200 Air Force personnel and 550 Naval personnel.

Alaska immediately became a defense area. All families of military personnel were ordered to leave. Only long-time residents of Alaska or persons on emergency business were permitted to travel from the States. All ships were ordered to remain in port. Censorship boards were set up to screen mail. Communications were placed under military censorship. A blackout was imposed in all cities. Gas masks were issued and civilian defense precautions were taken. Guards were assigned to watch for possible sabotage. All Japanese-Americans were sent south to detention camps to prevent possible espionage. Automobile sales were stopped and tires were rationed. Alaska was in the grip of the same war fever that afflicted the West Coast of the United States.

It would be more than 20 months before Alaskans relaxed, confident that the threat of enemy attack had been lifted.

---

[6]Gruening was a newspaper editor prior to being appointed governor by President Roosevelt.

The first troops to arrive in Alaska for the World War II military buildup wait to leave the Alaska Railroad yards in Anchorage on June 27, 1940. AHFAM

Units of the U.S. Navy's torpedo fleet lie up at the White Pass dock at Skagway in 1901. YA

Navy PBYs visit the Kodiak harbor on July 23, 1937, three years before the start of construction of the naval base there. NA

Newspapers around the country announced the formal entry of the United States into World War II.

SC

U. NAVAL AIR STATION, KODIAK, ALASKA
NAVAL COMMUNICATIONS

Original

Heading NFC NR 63 F L Z 75L 071830 C8Q TAR1 0 81   Date 7 DEC 41

From: CINCPAC

ALL SHIPS PRESENT AT HAWAIIN AREA.

To: URGENT

Info: DEFERRED unless otherwise checked | ROUTINE | PRIORITY | AIRMAIL | MAILGRAM

AIRRAID ON REARLHARBOR X THIS IS NO DRILL

07014

RM 58 1910 7DEC

U. NAVAL AIR STATION, KODIAK, ALASKA
NAVAL COMMUNICATIONS

Original

Heading NPC NR93F// L Z PARD 072334 SNAG P GR36 BT

From: COMDT 13TH NAVDIST

To: ASTA 13TH NAVDIST

Info: Date 7 DEC 1941 GCT

DEFERRED unless otherwise checked | ROUTINE | PRIORITY XXX | AIRMAIL | MAILGRAM

UNTIL FURTHER INSTRUCTIONS ARE ISSUED   ALL PLANES FLYING
OVER NAVAL STATIONS OTHER THAN AIR STATIONS WILL BE REGARDED
AS HOUTILE AND WILL BE FIRED ON WITHOUT WARNING X GIVE WIDE-
ST PUBLICITY
X THIS IS SNAG FOUR

08001

58 KCS HB AT 0015/8TH

U. NAVAL AIR STATION, KODIAK, ALASKA
NAVAL COMMUNICATIONS

Original

Heading NPC NR143F// L Z SNOW 081940 TEND ZRK GR131 BT   Date 9 DEC 1941 GCT

From: SECNAV

To: TO ALLNAVSTAS

Info: DEFERRED unless otherwise checked | ROUTINE | PRIORITY | AIRMAIL | MAILGRAM

THE ENEMY HAS STRUCK A SAVAGE COMMA TREACHEROUS BLOW X WE ARE AT
WAR COMMA ALL OF US EXCLAMATION POINT THERE IS NO TIME NOW FOR
DISPUTES OR DELAY OF ANY KIND X WE MUST HAVE   SHIPS AND
MORE SHIPS COMMA GUNS AND MORE GUNS COMMA MEN AND MORE MEN DASH
FASTER AND FASTER X THERE IS NO TIME TO LOSE X THE NAVY MUST LEAD 7W
THE WAY X SPEED UP DASH IT IS YOUR NAVY AND YOUR NATION EXCLAMAT-
ION POINT SIGNED FRANK KNOX SECRETARY OF THE NAVY X PARAGRAPH
X NAVAL ACRIVITIES WILL POST ON ALL BULLETIN BOARDS INSPECTORS WILL
REQUEST MAXIMUM PUBLICITY BY NAVAL CONTRACTORS X ALL SUGGESTIONS FOR
THE REMOVAL OF RESTRICTIONS OF EVERY NATURE WHICH WILL ELIMINATE
OR TEND TO ELIMINATE DELAY IN PRODUCTION WILL BE WELCOME.

1705 HB ON 58 KCS.

09035

The word of the Pearl Harbor attack was flashed to Alaska immediately.

Naval Archives, Seattle

P-40 fighter planes at the Northwest Staging Route airfield, Fort Nelson, British Columbia in 1942.

USA

NORTHWEST
STAGING ROUTE
CANADA FIGHTS BACK

When Canada entered World War II in September 1939, it directed its attention to the Atlantic and Europe, giving little thought to its Western defenses.

The Dominion nevertheless authorized planning for a number of airfields that would stretch from northern Alberta to Whitehorse, Yukon. After the Canadian-American Permanent Joint Board on Defense was created in August 1940, Canada authorized construction of these fields and two others at Prince George and Smithers, British Columbia, to provide access to Prince Rupert on the West Coast.

These airfields would provide protection, permit aircraft to be deployed rapidly to northwestern Canada and Alaska in time of emergency, and allow men and supplies to be moved into the region by air. In 1941 construction began at Grande Prairie, Alberta; Fort St. John and Fort Nelson, British Columbia, and Watson Lake and Whitehorse, Yukon.

The region north and west of Edmonton was almost totally wilderness, with few settlements or travelers. Some civilian air routes had been established, but the main form of transportation was still boat, and this was available only in summer. Hence, construction crews had to go into Fort St. John and Fort Nelson by the winter haul road from Dawson Creek, and supplies for Watson Lake were taken up the Stikine River from Wrangell, Alaska, to Telegraph Creek, Dease Lake, Dease River to Lower Post, just south of Watson Lake. Supplies for Whitehorse were brought in over the White Pass and Yukon Railroad.

At Edmonton, the southern terminus for the route, the Municipal Airport was expanded. This field became the focal point for shipments of planes, men and material to the North. Ladd Field near Fairbanks became the northern terminus of the international air route.

By the end of 1941 all airfields had been established, at least for daylight use. Their facilities were limited. With the United States' entry into war, they were upgraded considerably to meet U.S. Army Air Force standards. Eight additional emergency flight strips were constructed along the route of the new Alaska Highway.

The airfields were used for supplying Russia under the Lend-Lease program. More than 8,000 planes were flown up the route to Fairbanks and Nome, and turned over to Russian pilots for the flight into Siberia and then to Russia's front against Germany.

The military airfield at Watson Lake, Yukon, 300 miles southeast of Whitehorse.   USA

C-47 Skytrains and P-39 fighter planes at the Edmonton Municipal Airport in June 1942, waiting to be flown to Alaska. PAA

C-47 Skytrains and B-24 Liberator bombers at the Edmonton Municipal Airport. PAA

The military airfield at Grande Prairie, Alberta between Edmonton and Dawson Creek.

AAC

The military airfield at Fort St. John, British Columbia, 50 miles north of Dawson Creek on the newly constructed Alaska Highway.

AAC

The military airfield at Fort Nelson, British Columbia, halfway between Dawson Creek and Watson Lake, Yukon, on the Alaska Highway. AAC

Operations offices at the Fort Nelson military airfield in March 1942. USA

Members of the 95th Engineers lay a corduroy road at MP 15, June 2, 1942.   USA

THE ALASKA HIGHWAY
ROAD IN THE WILDERNESS

An overland route to Alaska had been dreamed of long before World War II. An American railroad builder, F. H. Harriman, proposed a Canada-Alaska railroad that would be linked to a Russian railroad by a bridge or tunnel at the Bering Straits. However, after the Russo-Japanese War of 1904, Japan pressured Russia into abandoning the idea.

In 1905, a Maj. Constantine of the North West Mounted Police was ordered to blaze an overland trail to the Klondike gold fields. He started from Fort St. John and got to the Stikine River before he was ordered back. He had built 375 miles of road.

Donald MacDonald, a United States government engineer, proposed an overland road to Alaska in 1928 as part of a route between the Polar Seas and Panama. This route could have served military purposes, but the country was not interested in military operations at that time.

In 1933, Congress authorized U.S. participation in a joint U.S.-Canadian commission to study a proposed road to Alaska. The commission was appointed, but did little in the 1930s.

With the start of the war, several routes were proposed.

The American members favored Route A, which started in central British Columbia at Prince George, then moved northwest to Hazelton, up the Stikine River to Atlin, to Teslin and Tagish Lakes, and to Whitehorse and Fairbanks via the Tanana Valley. The route would connect Alaska and Seattle and parallel the West Coast for 150 miles. It was vulnerable to attack from the sea and had steep grades and heavy snowfall. There were no air bases along the way.

The Canadians favored Route B, which also started at Prince George but which followed the Rocky Mountain Trench up the valleys of the Parsnip and Finlay Rivers to Finlay Forks and Syton Pass, then north to Francis Lake in the Yukon to the Pelly River. From there it went to Dawson City and down the Yukon Valley to connect with the Richardson Highway to Fairbanks. The advantage of this route was that it was farther inland, away from enemy planes. Again there were no air bases, however, and the route bypassed Whitehorse, an important town in the Yukon. The construction cost was estimated at $25 million, construction time at five to six years.

Vihjalmur Stefansson, the pioneer Arctic explorer, had proposed a Mackenzie River route from Great Slave Lake in the Northwest Territories down the Mackenzie River and across the Yukon Territory to Eagle, Alaska and Fairbanks. This route was considered impractical because of the remoteness of the area.

As it turned out, the so-called Prairie Route (Route C), advocated by the United States Army Corps of Engineers, was ruled the only practical one. It was far enough inland to avoid attack by enemy planes and it connected the vital air bases of the Northwest Staging Route from Edmonton to Whitehorse. It traversed more level terrain, going no higher than 4,250 feet. There was also a railhead at Dawson Creek, British Columbia, and a winter trail from there to Fort Nelson, 300 miles to the northwest. Other access points were through Skagway, Valdez and Seward, Alaska.

The road, when completed, stretched over 1,400 miles from Dawson Creek to its junction with the Richardson Highway at Delta Junction, Alaska.

The bombing of Pearl Harbor in 1941 was to produce one of the great engineering feats of the century. The West Coast of the United States and Canada and all of Alaska lay open to a possible Japanese invasion. Defense of the area was of paramount importance in the early days of the war.

The attack had prompted President Roosevelt to form a special Cabinet committee to study the problems of building a road to Alaska through Canada. Brig. Gen. C. L. Sturdevant, assistant chief of the U.S. Army Corps of Engineers, was assigned to plan the road's construction. Even after Pearl Harbor there was opposition to building the road. The Navy thought it could keep the sea lanes free of enemy intrusions and the Army questioned the use of badly needed supplies and soldiers on such a large-scale project. But the pressing need for a quick decision to get men and supplies to the area while the ground was still frozen prompted action. After much haggling over which route to follow, a decision was made on Feb. 2, 1942, to follow Route C, the Prairie Route. The order to start work was issued Feb. 14.

The plan was to start a road from the end of the railroad at Dawson Creek, British Columbia, cutting a pioneer road suitable only for military traffic to Whitehorse and terminating at Fairbanks. It was to be built as quickly as possible. Later it was to become a year-round road, with wider roadbeds and permanent bridges built by the U.S. Public Roads Administration (PRA).

Canadian cooperation was needed because most of the road would be built through British Columbia and the Yukon Territory. The Canadians agreed to furnish the right of way; to waive import duties, sales taxes, income taxes and immigration regulations, and to permit the taking of timber, gravel and rock along the route. The Americans agreed to pay for the construction and to turn over the Canadian portion of the road to the Canadian government six months after the war ended.

The first commander of the constructin project was Brig. Gen. William M. Hoge, who tried to control the entire length of the route. He set up a southern sector headquarters at Fort St. John and a northern sector headquarters at Whitehorse. This arrangement did not work because of the scope of the project, and in June Gen. Hoge assumed command of the northern sector while Col. James A. O'Connor took over the southern sector. O'Connor, a 1907 West Point graduate, was the engineer in charge of tunneling Corregidor's fortress in Manila harbor. Because of the need for overall control of construction and supply, a Northwest Service Command was established in September 1942 in Whitehorse with O'Connor, now a brigadier general, in charge. The command was responsible for all U.S. Army activities in that part of Canada, including the highway.

The road was initially named the Alcan Highway. Emergency funds were allocated and orders were issued to Army troops to proceed to the end of rail at Dawson Creek. On March 2, 1942, the first train carrying troops arrived at the town.

There were few reliable maps of the proposed route and only a few trails cut by local trappers and prospectors. There was a winter trail from Dawson Creek to Fort Nelson and a wagon road from Whitehorse northwest to Kluane Lake, but not much more.

The 35th Combat Engineer Regiment was ordered to proceed to Dawson Creek and then to Fort Nelson to begin location work in the spring. The 340th General Service Regiment went to Whitehorse and was to build the road south. The 341st General Service Regiment was stationed at Fort St. John and was to build the road to Fort Nelson. The 18th Combat Engineer Regiment went to Skagway and traveled the railroad to Whitehorse to build the road northwest toward Alaska.

Those four regiments were thus poised in the spring of 1942 for the great construction job ahead. Twelve hundred miles of road in Canada and more than 200 miles in Alaska were to be cut through as quickly as possible. With the addition of three more Army Engineer regiments, the 93rd, 95th and 97th--all of which were composed of black troops with white officers--the total strength of troops for the construction job in 1942 was more than 11,000. The Public Roads Administration provided location crews and private contractors.

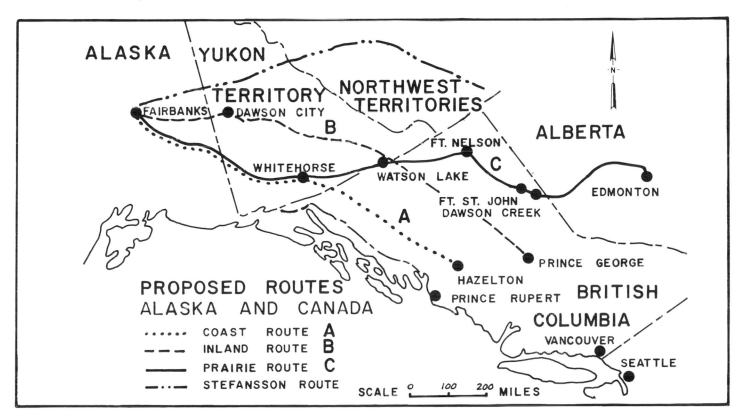

Map 2
Proposed routes for the Alaska Highway project.

17

Dawson Creek in early March was swarming with troops starting up the "road" to Fort St. John and Fort Nelson. The road was to follow the winter trail from Fort St. John past Charlie Lake through thick forests and along ridgetops on the eastern slopes of the Rocky Mountains, crossing several large rivers and continuing to Fort Nelson.

Local trappers, Indians and prospectors were pressed into service to help locate the way, although their suggestions for possible routes were not always the most appropriate for a motorized highway. Local packers with their mule teams were used to help supply the advance survey parties.

Three hundred thirty-five miles of wilderness stretched from Fort Nelson to Watson Lake, the first settlement in the Yukon Territory. The highest point of the road crossed Summit Lake at more than 4,000 feet. The road then went up mountains and down valleys, crossing rivers and hundreds of small streams. The road followed a general northwesterly direction to Watson Lake. Names such as Trutch, Steamboat Mountain, Toad River, Muncho Lake and the Liard River were etched forever in the minds of the soldiers who labored on the road.

At Lower Post, just south of the Yukon border,

the new road followed an old road to Watson Lake, where the route to the northwest was unclear. Several routes to Whitehorse were explored. The one finally chosen followed the Rancheria River Valley across the Mackenzie-Yukon River divide, then along the Swift River to Teslin Lake and Marsh Lake. It followed an old prospector's trail to Whitehorse.

From Whitehorse, the road skirted the north side of the St. Elias Range, went around the south shore of Kluane Lake, the largest in the Yukon, and crossed the large glacial rivers of the western Yukon--the Slims, the Donjek and the White.

At the Alaska border, more than 1,200 miles from Dawson Creek, the route went through the Tanana River Valley connecting Northway and Tok to Delta Junction, where it connected with the Richardson Highway, built in the early 1900s. Delta Junction is recognized by some, and Fairbanks by others, as the official end of the highway.

The soldiers of the Army and the civilians of the PRA faced countless days of below zero temperatures, snow, rain, insects and even intense heat.

By April, road locators were working throughout the country with the hum of bulldozers on their heels. Decisions on the route were sometimes

Members of the 341st Engineers stake out tents at their bivouac site at Dawson Creek, British Columbia, on May 1, 1942. The first troops had arrived in town in early March to begin the construction of the Alaska Highway. USA

18

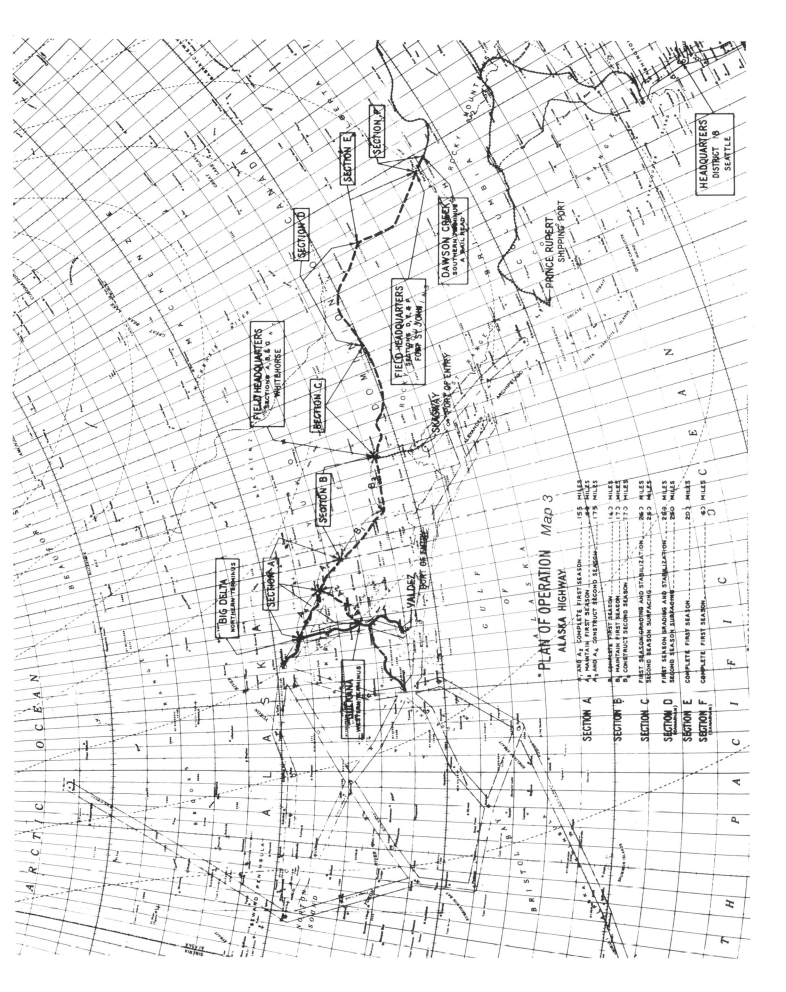

*PLAN OF OPERATION Map 3
ALASKA HIGHWAY

SECTION A	A_1 AND A_2 COMPLETE FIRST SEASON	155 MILES
	A_3 MAINTAIN FIRST SEASON	140 MILES
	A_3 AND A_4 CONSTRUCT SECOND SEASON	175 MILES
SECTION B	B_1 COMPLETE FIRST SEASON	140 MILES
	B_2 MAINTAIN FIRST SEASON	170 MILES
	B_3 CONSTRUCT SECOND SEASON	170 MILES
SECTION C	FIRST SEASON GRADING AND STABILIZATION	250 MILES
	SECOND SEASON SURFACING	250 MILES
SECTION D (CANADIAN)	FIRST SEASON GRADING AND STABILIZATION	240 MILES
	SECOND SEASON SURFACING	250 MILES
SECTION E	COMPLETE FIRST SEASON	203 MILES
SECTION F (CANADIAN)	COMPLETE FIRST SEASON	60 MILES C

BIG DELTA
NORTHERN TERMINUS

SECTION A

PRINCE WILLIAM
WESTERN TERMINUS

VALDEZ
PORT OF ENTRY

SECTION B

SECTION C

FIELD HEADQUARTERS
SECTIONS A, B, & C
WHITEHORSE

SECTION G

FIELD HEADQUARTERS
SECTIONS D, E, & F
FORT ST. JOHN

SKAGWAY
CANADIAN PORT OF ENTRY

SECTION D

SECTION E

SECTION F

DAWSON CREEK
SOUTHERN TERMINUS
& RAIL HEAD

PRINCE RUPERT
SHIPPING PORT

HEADQUARTERS
DISTRICT 18
SEATTLE

19

made on the spot and if the route was not quite in the right place, the PRA men corrected it later. Workers often climbed trees to figure out the route ahead. Then the bulldozers would cut out a path. Often three to four miles of road were built in a day as the summer daylight hours permitted the men to work 24 hours a day. The big push was to get to Fairbanks as soon as possible with a pioneer road. Local bush pilots were hired to ferry men and supplies along the route. The riverboats along the Yukon's inland rivers and lakes were pressed into service. No limit was set on the amount of equipment or money used. To the old-timers of the North, this explosion of American power and wealth was overwhelming.

There was a race against time in the southern sector, as spring thaws made travel over the winter trail in the Fort St. John to Fort Nelson area impossible. Supplies had to be stockpiled on the route for the spring and summer construction period.

The most pressing problem along the route was the inexperience of the engineers in building a highway on the muskeg and permafrost. The ground is permanently frozen just below the surface in many areas along the route, and if the top layer is stripped off, the underlying ground thaws and produces a quagmire. Ditches were dug to drain off the water, but these were usually ineffective. Finally the crews

left the muskeg intact and built the road on top of it, laying a roadbed of gravel where needed.

The construction methods took a terrific toll in men and machines, and there were many accidents. One of the worst was at Charlie Lake near Fort St. John on May 14, 1942. Eleven men drowned in the lake when their raft capsized. Other men were killed in road accidents or died from the extreme cold.

The route between Whitehorse and the Alaska border was extremely hard to work on. Information was inadequate and the terrain was difficult. There were miles of swamps and large glacial rivers to cross, and much hardrock construction was required, especially around Kluane Lake. Ice jams in the rivers during the spring breakup were dangerous. The temperatures in the winter fell to 50 degrees and more below zero. At this temperature, machinery would not function and it was dangerous to work outdoors. But work continued through the early spring, summer and fall, and the road inched toward Alaska. The troops were building both north and south of Whitehorse, the major supply point of the northern sector, and toward Whitehorse from Fort Nelson. Additional troops of the 97th Engineers proceeded north from Valdez, Alaska, and started building the road southeast to the Yukon border. PRA and Alaska Road Commission personnel also worked to improve the Richardson Highway into Fairbanks.

A pack train takes supplies to the forward road locators and surveyors.　　　USA

20

Gov. Ernest Gruening of Alaska, second from left, at U.S. Army Engineers headquarters in White-horse in October 1942. On the left is Brig. Gen. James A. O'Connor, commanding general of the highway construction. Third from the left is Col. John Wheeler, in charge of the actual construction work, and at the right is Col. K. Bush, Chief of Staff.   *NA*

Finally, on Sept. 24, 1942, bulldozer operators of the 35th and 340th regiments met at Contact Creek (MP 588.1, Km 946.3) to close the southern sector of the road. On Oct. 20, troops working south from Alaska and north from Whitehorse met at Beaver Creek, Yukon (MP 1202, Km 1934). The pioneer road had been completed in the record time of eight months and 12 days. An opening ceremony was held at Soldiers Summit on Kluane Lake on Nov. 20, 1942. Gen. O'Connor represented the U.S. Army and Ian Mackenzie represented Canada. The joint effort of the two countries probably would not have been undertaken for many years except for the war.

But this was only the beginning, because the pioneer road was just that--a pioneer road, very rough, part of it only one lane wide, that would have to be improved immediately to be useful to the increasing military traffic.

One of the biggest problems for the construction men was bridging the many small streams and major rivers along the route. Over the entire stretch of highway 133 bridges and 8,000 culverts were built. Some of the streams could be crossed with small log structures, but not the meandering glacier-fed rivers, hundreds of yards wide, that turned into raging torrents during spring breakup. Those rivers called for advanced bridge building techniques.

Temporary log or pontoon bridges were constructed over the smaller streams, and ferries were used on the larger rivers. Later PRA personnel improved bridges as well as the road.

The Donjek River northwest of Kluane Lake was the hardest to cross. It is a wide, braided, glacial river whose spring floods and ice jams play havoc with bridge abutments. The White River 40 miles further up the road, is another raging glacial river. Several successive log structures were stretched across the rivers but nothing was really satisfactory until permanent structures were built.

The original Nisutlin Bay Bridge at Teslin Lake was the longest trestle bridge, stretching more than 2,300 feet. The pilings for the foundations were set on thin layers of sand in the river bottom, which was mostly solid ice.

The Peace River bridge at Taylor near Fort St. John was the most difficult one to build. A ferry was used to carry supplies across the river, but it was not adequate. A timber trestle bridge was built in October 1942, but the river destroyed it in November. A permanent steel bridge was started in December 1942 and completed in August

1943. It was 2,130 feet long. The river, however, was very treacherous in this area and it kept hammering at the piers until part of the bridge collapsed on Oct. 16, 1957. The government began to plan a new bridge at once and the present one was opened in January 1960.

Building a road in that remote part of the continent was very difficult for men and machines. The pressure to finish it as soon as possible did not leave much time for recreation or admiring the scenery. Thousands of men were suddenly moved to a hostile environment in which they had to contend with cold, substandard quarters, loneliness, insects, fatigue, dangerous construction methods, and few facilities for recreation. The black soldiers had the most difficult time, for most were from the South and could not get used to the sub-zero temperatures. Despite all this, the troops did an admirable job.

Living conditions were particularly bad in the early period of construction. Men lived in tents with insufficient heat in the winter and little insect protection in the summer. Supplying food for so many troops was another problem. As highway construction progressed, more suitable quarters were built and the food got better. In the winter, moose were abundant and provided a delightful alternative to canned meat.

Insects were a major problem because of the large expanses of water in which they lived. Head nets were common, especially during the summer. Many a man was unable to work because of swelling from insect bites.

The cold was probably the hardest thing to get used to. Most of the men had never experienced such extreme temperature ranges and in the worst of the cold it was dangerous to work around the machines. Flesh could freeze to metal in seconds. A fall from a bridge meant a plunge into ice water.

After the pioneer road was punched through the wilderness, the PRA began improving it to make it passable year-round with widths of 26 to 32 feet. Grades were reduced and straightened, new roadbeds were built across the many swampy sections and permanent bridges were constructed. The same problems that faced the builders of the pioneer road also confronted the PRA men.

As the original Army construction regiments were pulled off the project in 1943, private contractors were hired by the PRA to do the reconstruction. They employed more than 16,000 civilian workers. PRA offices were set up in Fort St. John and Whitehorse to direct the construction, and other small offices were scattered along the route.

Map makers and surveyors work at a plane table ahead of the construction crews. USA

Camp and administration buildings for U.S. Army Engineers at Fort St. John, British Columbia, in May 1942. Fort St. John was the Field Headquarters for highway construction between Dawson Creek and Watson Lake. GAI

Headquarters for the Whitehorse Sector of the Alaska Highway construction project in June 1942. American officers pose in front of the building. USA

Five major contractors were hired to oversee the construction. Each in turn subcontracted with individual companies for certain parts of the job. In addition, highly technical contractors were hired for the large bridge projects. Because of variable weather and supply problems, no one had any idea how long it would take to bring the road up to a standard for safe travel.

More than 70 companies were involved in the reconstruction project, and in October 1943, with the military situation improving in the Pacific area and the highway upgraded as an all-weather road, the government ordered the project completed. Thousands of men and tons of material and machines started to move to the "outside." The Army then took over and did the maintenance necessary to keep the road open.

The road cost more than $135 million.

The Haines Cutoff road was authorized by the U. S. Army in November 1942, as the Alaska Pioneer Road was being finished. The cutoff was to be built to link the port of Haines, Alaska, with the Alaska Highway, a distance of 160 miles. It was built to provide an alternate route to the highway in case the White Pass and Yukon Railroad should be blocked, to provide another port for the shipment of supplies to the highway and to provide a possible mass evacuation route from Alaska.

The road was built between January and December 1943 at a cost of more than $13 million. It traverses the rugged country on the east side of the St. Elias Range through parts of Alaska, British Columbia and the Yukon Territory.

Some of the construction difficulties encountered on the Alaska Highway were also met on the cutoff road, but much had been learned on the original pioneer road. Camps were built along the route for the construction workers. Major camps were at 103-Mile and Dezadeash Lake.

In the winter of 1944, the U.S. Army discontinued winter maintenance of the road.

By the latter part of 1943 the threat of a Japanese invasion had waned. The highway was not needed as critically as it had been during the early days of 1942. The U.S. Army was responsible for maintenance of the road, but by 1944, the work force had been reduced to between 300 and 500 men, all Canadian civilians. The idea of building an all-weather highway with high standards was abandoned for the time being and only essential relocation work was authorized. All work by the PRA had been phased out by the end of October 1943.

The problems encountered by the initial construction crews, especially icing and washouts, were inherited by the civilian workers. Bridges were a continual problem; dozens were washed out in 1943 and 1944. It was a constant battle to keep the highway open with the adverse weather conditions, limited funding and manpower.

Six months after the war ended the highway was turned over to Canadian authorities.

A ferry on the Peace River at Taylor Flats near Fort St. John. This was one of the largest river crossings on the highway and was finally bridged in August 1943.   GAI

Chow tables were built and then moved along with everything else each time a new campsite was established. The wide-brimmed campaign hats were used in the summer so mosquito nets could be draped over them to cover the head and shoulder. YA

The 18th Engineer Regiment's band gives a concert at the Silver City Camp on Kluane Lake, Yukon, on July 4, 1942. YA

Log bridges were built across the many stream crossings. More permanent structures would be built later.
YA

Troops build a log bridge. Cross-cut saws were the power saws of the day. Native material close at hand was used to cross many streams.
USA

The highway was a pioneer road that had many steep grades and curves like this one. It would be up to the civilian construction crews to make this into an all-weather road. Four-wheeled drive was a must on most sections of the road.   *USA*

Catel (Canadian Telephone) trucks on one of the highways in the North Country. A telephone line was built between Edmonton and Fairbanks using the right-of-way of the Alaska and Canol highways.   *Russell Gettleman, Green Bay, Wisc.*

Large bulldozers bogged down in the mud.   USA

The Sikanni Chief Bridge at Mile Post 117, the first bridge reconstructed in 1943. After the pioneer road was completed in November 1942 the PRA came through and reconstructed part of the road and many of the bridges.

USA

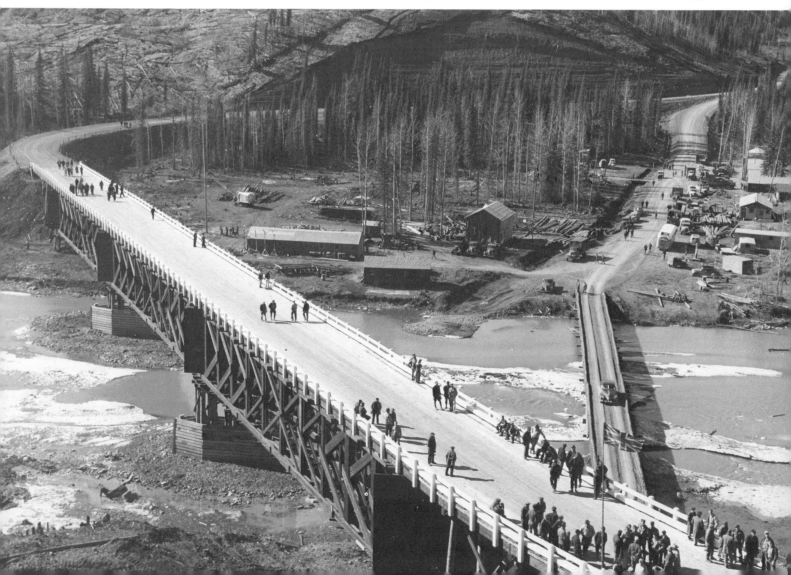

A broad street in a typical construction camp.   YA

The camp of the 18th Engineer Regiment in Whitehorse in 1942.   YA

Aircraft were used extensively for reconnaissance and supply along the highway route. This float plane landed along the shore of Kluane Lake in the summer of 1942.　　　YA

Army vehicles and equipment are loaded onto barges at the Dawson City dock in 1942. They were taken down the Yukon and Tanana Rivers to Fairbanks for use on the Richardson Highway.　The sternwheelers **Klondike** and **White Horse** are visible behind the barges.　　　YA

The first convoy in route from Whitehorse to Fairbanks in late November 1942, eight months after construction had begun. YA

The opening ceremony at Soldiers Summit above Kluane Lake, Yukon, on Nov. 20, 1942. The temperature was 30° below zero. NA

Buildings at the Whitehorse refinery area. This entire plant was dismantled in Texas, shipped by rail to Prince Rupert, B.C., put on ships to Skagway and transferred by rail again to Whitehorse, where it was reconstructed. It received its first crude oil from Norman Wells in April 1944.

USA

THE CANOL PROJECT
PIPELINE IN THE WILDERNESS

A dependable supply of fuel is esential to any army. The build-up of arms and men in Alaska and northwestern Canada before and after Pearl Harbor was totally dependent upon fuel from outside the area.

Most of the petroleum products had to be hauled up the Inside Passageway to Skagway, Alaska, or across the open seas to Seward, Alaska, and then transshipped by rail to the interior of Alaska and Yukon.

When the Northwest Staging Route was built in Canada, aviation fuel had to be flown in or hauled by winter sled trains to the isolated areas.

None of these methods of fuel transportation was completely satisfactory because of the manpower problems in handling the individual 55-gallon drums and the threat of Japanese airplanes and submarines to the shipping lanes. Once the Alaska Highway was opened in November 1942, some fuel shipments could be made by truck, but the "pioneer" road could not carry heavy truck traffic.

A possible source of oil was at a remote site on the Mackenzie River in Canada's Northwest Territories known as Norman Wells. It was 75 miles south of the Arctic Circle and 52 miles downstream from the old trading post of Fort Norman. An oilfield had been discovered and developed in 1920, with four producing wells and a small refinery, built in 1939, to supply local needs. The refined products were shipped by barge on the Mackenzie River. The site was simply too remote to supply the expanding needs of the military, being more than 1,000 miles from the nearest railhead by way of several rivers and lakes that were ice free only a few months each year.

In its push to obtain a dependable source of fuel, the U.S. Army proposed building a pipeline from Norman Wells on the east bank of the Mackenzie River south and west to Whitehorse, Yukon, a distance of nearly 500 miles. At Whitehorse a refinery would be built and the refined product could then be hauled up and down the Alaska Highway.

This was an enormous undertaking. Not only was there unmapped wilderness betwen the two points, but along with the pipeline, a road would have to be built to haul in the supplies. This was a job comparable to the Alaska Highway construction project.

The Canol (short for Canadian Oil) Project would be built and paid for by the U.S. Army with the consent of Canada. A consortium of American companies was formed to construct the road and pipeline. Known as BPC, it was composed of the W. A. Bechtel Company of San Francisco, the H. C. Price Company of Bartlesville, Oklahoma, and the W. E. Callahan Company of Dallas, Texas. (Several small subsidiaries of these companies were also involved.) The work was directed by the U.S. Army Corps of Engineers. Col. Theodore Wyman was put in command and in March 1943 was succeeded by Brig. Gen. L. D. Worsham. In December 1943 the Canol Project was placed under the Northwest Service Command. The Standard Oil Company of California would operate the pipeline and the refinery at Whitehorse and the Imperial Oil Company of Canada would produce the oil at Norman Wells.

It took 20 months, from June 1942 to April 1944, to get oil flowing into Whitehorse.[1]

Since the only access to the oil fields was by

---

[1]On May 20, 1942, a United States War Department contract was signed in Washington on the recommendation of the Canada-United States Permanent Joint Defense Board. This authorized construction.

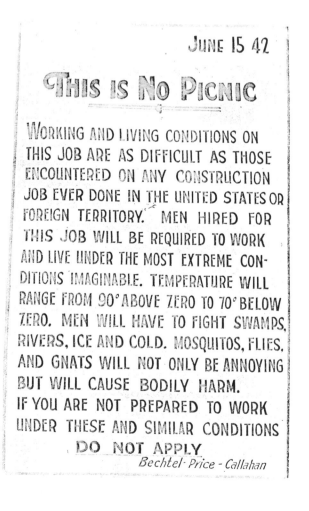

Sign at the Edmonton employment office of Bechtel-Price-Callahan, the prime contractor for the Canol Project. YA

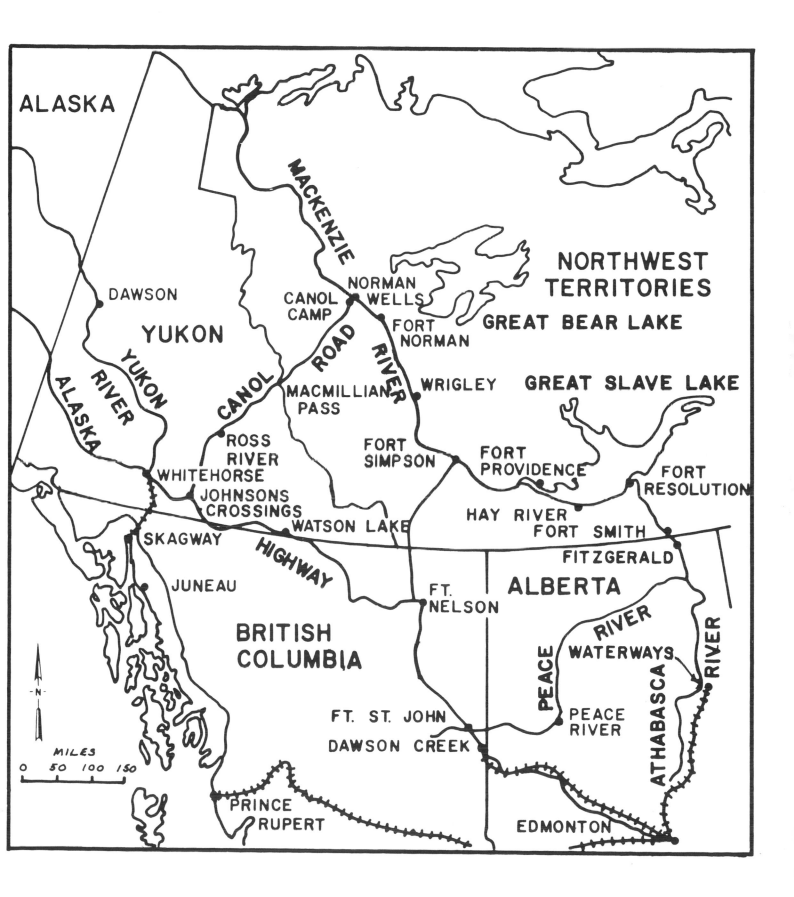

ALASKA

YUKON

DAWSON

YUKON RIVER

ALASKA

MACKENZIE

NORTHWEST
TERRITORIES

GREAT BEAR LAKE

NORMAN
WELLS

CANOL
CAMP

FORT
NORMAN

ROAD

RIVER

CANOL

MACMILLIAN
PASS

WRIGLEY

GREAT SLAVE LAKE

ROSS
RIVER

FORT
SIMPSON

FORT
PROVIDENCE

FORT
RESOLUTION

WHITEHORSE

JOHNSONS
CROSSINGS

HAY RIVER

FORT SMITH

WATSON LAKE

FITZGERALD

SKAGWAY

HIGHWAY

FT.
NELSON

ALBERTA

JUNEAU

BRITISH
COLUMBIA

PEACE

RIVER

WATERWAYS

ATHABASCA

RIVER

FT. ST. JOHN

DAWSON CREEK

PEACE
RIVER

N

MILES
0   50   100 150

PRINCE
RUPERT

EDMONTON

Map 4
The Canol Project.

35

the Mackenzie River, a whole new group of roads and airfields had to be built before the road-pipe-line construction project could begin.

BPC crews established a camp at Waterways, 285 miles north of Edmonton, at the end of the railhead. From here supplies could be shipped down the Athabaska, Slave and Mackenzie rivers and Great Slave Lake to Norman Wells, a distance of over 1,400 miles. A boat trip downstream by this route could take 14 to 18 days. Sixty to seventy thousand tons of supplies were shipped this way between 1942 and 1944, using every conceivable type of barge and boat. Even old sternwheelers from the Hudson's Bay Company were pressed into service. Supplies could be hauled from May until the rivers iced up, usually in October.

Canol Camp, directly across the Mackenzie River from Norman Wells, was established with a work force of 1,000 men. From here the road-pipeline would be built to connect with the Alaska Highway 400 miles to the southwest.[2]

At Slave River, 285 miles north of Waterways, the river dropped 16 feet with strong rapids, so at Fort Fitzgerald everything had to be unloaded

[2]The actual length of the road-pipeline was 577 miles due to many detours encountered.

from the boats and portaged around the obstruction.

Ten airfields were constructed from Edmonton north to Norman Wells. The first plane landed at Norman Wells in September 1942. Construction camps were established at Waterways, Fort Fitzgerald, Fort Smith, the Slave Delta, Fort Resolution, Hay River, Wrigley Harbor, Fort Providence, Fort Simpson, Fort Wrigley, Norman Wells and Canol Camp. The supply lines for the project aggregated more than 9,000 miles.

Roads had to be built from northern Alberta just to get equipment to the Canol Camp. A 1,000 mile winter haul road was constructed from Peace River, Alberta, to Norman Wells, and an all-weather road was constructed northward from Peace River to the Mackenzie River. It was opened by BPC on Feb. 23, 1943. A road was also constructed from just north of Fort Nelson on the Alaska Highway, north to Fort Simpson on the Mackenzie River.

The entire North Country was gearing up for the two massive construction projects--the Alaska Highway and the Canol Project. At Prince Rupert, British Columbia, on the Pacific Coast, new loading docks, warehouses, barracks and storage tanks were built so equipment could be brought there by

A GI band playing outdoors at Fort Smith, Northwest Territories, in 1942.   GAI

36

GIs of the Canol Project gather in a store at Fort Resolution, Northwest Territories, in 1942.

GAI

train and then shipped north by boat to Skagway, Alaska. Skagway at the head of the Lynn Canal and the southern terminus for the White Pass and Yukon Railroad was already taxed beyond its capacity, hauling supplies for the Alaska Highway.

The Canol road, which had to be built first in order to move in the pipeline material, was a very difficult construction project. Ahead of the construction crews lay over 400 miles of complete wilderness, some of it never traversed by man. An air reconnaissance was made first to determine a feasible route across the Mackenzie Mountains. With local Indians as guides, traverses were made by dog team. The road builders followed in tractor trains from Canol Camp, blazing a trail across the Mackenzie Range.

The road-pipeline would cross Macmillan Pass at the Northwest Territories-Yukon border, then down the Ross River Valley, crossing the South Fork and Anvil Range to a connection with the Alaska Highway at Johnson's Crossing.

After the Japanese occupied several Aleutian Islands in June 1942, the U.S. Army decided to speed up the construction and in February 1943, construction on the road started from the west. Seven months later the crews linked the east and west sections together. In August 1943, the U.S. Army engineers were needed elsewhere so BPC crews completed the road.

Pipe layers followed the road crews and laid a four-inch line, switching to six-inch for the final 110 miles. The pipe came in 20- to 22-foot sections weighing 230 pounds each.[3] The sections had to be welded together, often in sub-freezing temperatures. More than a hundred rivers and streams had to be crossed and three lines were buried across the four-mile-wide Mackenzie River from Norman Wells to Canol Camp. Ten pumping stations were built between Canol Camp and Whitehorse, their diesel engines being fueled by crude oil taken from the pipeline.

While the road-pipeline were being constructed, work began on the refinery in Whitehorse. A refinery in Texas was dismantled and shipped by rail to Prince Rupert, by ship to Skagway and by rail to Whitehorse. Work started on the refinery site in April 1943 on the Lewes River (part of the Yukon) just below the town. Eighteen 10,000-gallon storage tanks were built to hold the crude oil. The refinery was completed in January 1944 and crude oil was flowing into it from Norman Wells in April.

In the meantime, 30 new wells were being drilled at the oilfield to increase production from 3,000 to 20,000 barrels a day. By October 1944, there were 51 producing wells in the field. Tank

---

[3]15,000 tons of pipe were needed for the 577-mile total pipeline length.

37

farms were being built at Norman Wells, Canol Camp and Whitehorse. Oil from the wells had a parrafin base and would flow at -70°F so the pipe could be laid on top of the ground with no worry about the extreme cold temperatures.

Since this whole project would take time to complete, an alternate source for the transport of petroleum products was needed. A four-inch pipeline along the White Pass Route was completed between Skagway and Whitehorse in January 1943. Fuel could now be brought up to Skagway and pumped to Whitehorse. Another two-inch line was begun in February 1943, tapping the original line and carrying fuel along the Alaska Highway to Watson Lake, 300 miles southeast of Whitehorse. This supplied the highway traffic and the airfields. It was in operation with four pumping stations by June 1943. Another three-inch line tapped the original line and was laid along the highway north for 600 miles to Fairbanks and Ladd Field. It was completed in November 1943 with 15 pumping stations in operation. Tank farms were constructed up and down the length of the Alaska Highway to hold this incoming fuel.

The Canol pipeline was completed on Feb. 16, 1944, and crude oil flowed into the Whitehorse refinery in April.[4] One of the longest open-wire telephone lines in the world had been strung between Fairbanks-Norman Wells and Helena, Montana, by February 1944. This line, over 3,000 miles long,

enabled the entire area to have reliable communications with the outside world.

By the time all projects had been completed in 1944, at a cost of more than $135 million, the usefulness of the project was questionable. The invasion scare was over, the Japanese had been driven out of the Aleutians and the enemy was being pushed back on all fronts. The U.S. War Department announced that it would discontinue operations at Canol on June 30, 1945.

At war's end the refinery at Whitehorse and the Canol road fell into disuse.[5] Delegate Anthony Dimond of Alaska termed the development of the Norman Wells field at a cost of more than $100 million "completely inexcusable." He believed the oil industry should have been developed in Alaska rather than in the Canadian Northwest.

In late 1943 the project was investigated by the War Production Board and the Senate's Truman Committee. They complained that the War Department had built the road-pipeline secretly and had made no provision for American rights and interests after the war.

However, the War Department declared that it was built in a wartime emergency and although not completed until after the Japanese threat had lessened considerably, it could still be helpful in a possible northern invasion of Japan.

There is no question, however, that the construction of the Canol road-pipeline and the Alaska Highway contributed greatly to the development of the North Country.

[4]Once the system was in full operation it was supposed to reduce the cost of aviation gas to one-quarter the cost of carrying it in trucks over the Highway and one-tenth the cost of flying it to the airfields.

[5]The Whitehorse refinery processed close to a million barrels of crude oil from the Norman Wells field in nearly a year of operation.

The refinery at Norman Wells, Northwest Territories, was built in 1939 to produce petroleum products for the area from the 21 producing wells in the field. SC

Tugs and barges beached for the winter at Norman Wells on the Mackenzie River, North-west Territories. YA

A ferry operates on a river between Grande Prairie and High Prairie in northern Alberta in 1944. USA

Camp #111 on the Canol Road in the Northwest Territories in 1944.   USA

A view of the Norman Wells Camp from the airport road.   YA

Construction on the Canol Road project in the Northwest Territories. YA

Canol road and pipeline. YA

PIPE
LINE

A Russian flight crew and an American officer in front of a lend-lease plane, 1942.
UAA

LEND-LEASE
TO RUSSIA
THE MONTANA-ALASKA-
RUSSIA CONNECTION

Germany's attack on Russia on June 22, 1941, changed the character of the war in Europe. The blitzkreig at first overwhelmed the Russians. Russia pleaded with her new ally, Britain, and with neutral America for help. In December 1941, the United States and Russia signed a lend-lease protocol.[1] Harry Hopkins, aide to President Roosevelt, flew to Moscow to promise Premier Stalin that aid was coming. On July 7, 1941, a Soviet delegation flew from Vladivostok to Nome and then to Kodiak and Seattle for secret talks at the Olympic Hotel with American officials. At first the United States turned over some destroyers at Cold Bay in Alaska to the Russians. Supplies were loaded on the West Coast for shipment to Siberian ports.

After Pearl Harbor, the United States could ship war materiel to Russia without being restricted by its technical status as a neutral.

Russia, which lost much of its air force in the first few months of the German onslaught, cried out for fighters and bombers to supplement the planes it was building. One of the two main routes for shipping planes and war materiel to Russia was the sea route across the North Atlantic and around the North Cape to the ice-free Arctic ports of Murmansk and Archangel. It was the shorter, but by far the more dangerous route. Most materiel was shipped this way into 1942. Ships had to be placed in heavily protected convoys, constantly threatened by German U-boats, surface raiders and aircraft stationed in Norway. The weather in this part of the world was terrible most of the year.

The other route was by ship across the Atlantic Ocean around the Cape of Good Hope of Africa and up to the Iranian port of Basra, where supplies were unloaded onto trains.[2] Planes were flown to South America, across the Atlantic Ocean to Africa, and then across the continent to Iran. After the Mediterranean Sea was secured, shipments went through the Suez Canal. Either way, it took too long to get goods to Russia and the desert sands ruined aircraft engines.

It was determined that the best route for planes would be via Alaska and Siberia. Although great distances were involved and the worst possible weather conditions would be encountered, the planes would be delivered in flying condition and the possibility of enemy action was remote.

The United States wanted to fly the planes directly to Siberia, where they would be handed over to the Russian Air Force. The Russians would not allow this, partly for fear of provoking a Japanese response and partly because they did not want Americans on their soil.[3] Actually, this route had been proposed in September 1941, but Stalin vetoed it. With losses mounting on the sea run to Murmansk and the great distances involved in the Middle East, the Russians finally agreed to open the Alaska-Siberia (known as ALSIB) air route on Aug. 3, 1942.

In May 1941, the Army Ferrying Command had been established at Long Beach, California, to speed up the transportation of aircraft throughout the world. In June 1942 the command was moved to Great Falls, Montana.[4] The first location there was Gore Field, the municipal airport of Great Falls, but construction was started on East Base, six miles from town. Soon afterward the 7th Ferrying Group of the Air Transport Command (ATC) was assigned to Gore Field and four months later moved to East Base. Its assignment was to establish an air route from Great Falls to Ladd Field near Fairbanks, Alaska. In November 1942, the Alaskan Wing of the ATC was established and the 34th Sub-Depot of the Air Service Command was set up to handle lend-lease materiel.

Planes were brought into Great Falls, winterized and then flown up the Northwest Staging Route airfields of Edmonton, Grand Prairie, Fort St. John, Fort Nelson, Watson Lake, Whitehorse to Ladd Field. Many auxiliary strips were constructed, including a major one at Galena on the Yukon River between Ladd and Nome.

A major airfield was built at Nome (Marks Air Force Base), the last stopping point for the planes before they left for Siberia. This field was to play an important part in the lend-lease program. Ladd was selected over Nome as the main northern base because it had better weather and was farther away from possible enemy attack.

Because of the terrible weather, the most difficult part of the air route was between White-

---

[1]Lend-lease agreements similar to the Russian protocol were signed with Great Britain, China, Belgium, Czechoslovakia, Ethiopia, Greece, Liberia, the Netherlands, Norway, Poland and Yugoslavia. Australia, New Zealand and Canada had also accepted most of the lend-lease terms.

[2]This route was more than 13,000 miles long compared to the Alaska route of 1,900 miles.

[3]The Japanese and Russians remained at peace until August 8, 1945, two days after the atomic bomb was dropped on Hiroshima. Stalin wanted to grab whatever territory he could without doing any fighting. He annexed the Kurile Islands and invaded Manchuria. He hoped Japan would be divided into occupied zones, as Germany had been, but this did not happen.

[4]It was discovered that Great Falls, at an elevation of 3,665 feet, had more than 300 clear flying days a year and was on a direct line by the Circle route from the United States to Russia.

horse and Ladd Field. The route north from Edmonton became known as the "Million Dollar Valley" because of the many crashes.

In the 21 months of the program, nearly 8,000 aircraft were sent through Great Falls for transfer to Russia. These included P-39 Aircobra fighters, P-63 Kingcobra fighters, P-40 Warhawk fighters, A-20 and B-25 bombers, C-47 Skytrain transports and AT-6 trainers. The fighters were flown mostly by contract pilots, but the medium bombers and transports had to be flown by instrument-rated Air Force personnel. Millions of pounds of aircraft parts, tools, explosives, medical supplies and other materials were shipped to Russia in the planes. Diplomatic and personal mail also was handled.

In October 1942, the ATC set up command at the Edmonton Municipal Airport. Northwest and Western Airlines got contracts to provide transport services along the ASLIB route. The first lend-lease plane left Great Falls for Alaska in August

The Russo-American Bureau of Information at the Nome Air Base. Although the Russian airmen were guests in Alaska they tended to remain aloof from the Americans   *UAA*

1942, but soon flights had to be reduced because Siberian airfields were not capable of receiving as many aircraft as the United States was providing.

In September 1942 the first Russians arrived in Alaska to set up a permanent command at Ladd Field and Nome. They were assigned to special areas of the bases and usually kept to themselves. At the height of the program there were anywhere from 150 to 600 Russian pilots at Ladd Field waiting for planes.

Russian insistence that the planes be in perfect condition before being flown to Siberia caused constant delays and some antagonism between the two commands. Living quarters had been hastily built and supplying them was a problem. The Russian pilots had to be trained quickly in the rudiments of flying their new American planes, and also had to learn tower procedures. Language problems caused delays. Once the Russians learned these procedures they flew the planes from Ladd and Nome to Novosibirsk in Siberia and then to the various fronts in western Russia. There were many crashes by the Russian pilots.

The winter of 1942-43 was extremely harsh in Alaska. Planes had to be winterized before they could be flown out. With temperatures at 40°

Russian pilots examine a lend-lease aircraft at Ladd Field.   *USAF*

to 70° below zero it was hard to work on the aircraft. Most had to be left outside the hangars, and it sometimes took hours to warm up a plane. It is a real tribute to the aircraft crews that they kept these planes flying.

In September 1945 the last plane was flown to Siberia. Since 1942, 133 planes had been lost to weather conditions or pilot error--only 1.6 percent of the 7,983 planes that had been delivered to the Russians.[5]

Looking back, it seems questionable that the Russians needed all these aircraft. By 1943, Russia was building a great number of planes in factories in the Ural Mountains. Some think the Russians used the air route to filter through the United States stolen American secrets, especially

information on the atomic bomb. Apparently some uranium was shipped through Great Falls and in May 1944 it was discovered that U.S. Treasury plates had gone up the air route. Never before had the U.S. government let its money-printing plates out of the country.

In all, $9.5 billion in war materiel and other supplies was shipped to Russia by the three major routes. Russia had a virtual blank check during the war and such non-military items as cigarette cases, records, women's compacts, fishing tackle, dolls, playground equipment, cosmetics and even 13,328 sets of false teeth were funneled through Great Falls. In addition, many complete factories and plans for others were sent, all in the name of lend-lease.[6]

---

[5]The number of planes delivered to Russia from Alaska was as follows: 1942, 148; 1943, 2,662; 1944, 3,164; 1945, 2,009.

---

[6]For an account of the various legal and supposedly illegal shipments of supplies to Russia read: **Major Jordan's Diaries,** by Major George Racey Jordan, Harcourt Brace Jovanovich, 1952.

An American maintenance man paints a Russian Red Star insignia on a lend-lease plane bound for Russia, September 1942.
USAF

46

East Base (now called Malmstrom Air Force Base) at Great Falls, Montana. This was the initial assembly point in the United States for the ferrying of Russian lend-lease planes to Alaska. The planes were partly or totally winterized here before being flown north.

USAF

Hangar at East Base.

USAF

Russian lend-lease aircraft lined up at Ladd Field near Fairbanks, Alaska. The top photograph shows Douglas A-20 bombers and the bottom photograph shows Bell P-39 fighters. The Red Star was painted on the aircraft before they were flown north from Great Falls.

USAF

This Russian war plane helped protect the first military mission to arrive in Alaska at Nome in the late summer of 1942. USAF

The first Russian military mission to Alaska arrives at Nome in the late summer of 1942. The soldiers in helmets and the officer in riding breeches are American; the rest are Russian. The Russian aircraft has been heavily camouflaged. USAF

P-63s and other lend-lease aircraft are lined up at the Nome Air Base before being flown to Siberia in 1945.

USAF

The military airfield at Nome, Alaska was built on the flats close to the Bering Sea. This was the last Alaskan airfield before Siberia. The town of Nome lies on the beach next to the field.

UAA

View of Nome with the airfield in the distance. A gold dredge is in the right background. The frozen Bering Sea is in the left foreground.

UAA

Russian and American "comrades" in 1942.   UAA

Severe weather conditions and the Russians' inexperience with U.S. planes caused many accidents. This bomber was wrecked on the edge of the runway at Nome.   UAA

Once in a while the bitter cold, fog, wind, and isolation of Nome were broken by a social activity. Here Russian and American officers and their partners dance at the officers' club.
USAF

At East Base, Great Falls, Montana, on Oct. 6, 1944, Russian Maj. Gen. Slavin boards a C-47 for his home journey to Moscow following the Dumbarton Oaks conference in Washington, D.C. Lt. George W. Lanschinski (back to camera), the Alaskan Division interpreter and a United Nations representative bid him and the other Russian delegates goodbye.
USAF

SEPTEMBER 1942

SEPTEMBER 1945

COLONEL M. G. MACHIM
SOVIET MILITARY MISSION IN ALASKA
SEPTEMBER 1942 — MAY 1944

COLONEL PETER KISILEV
CO, SOVIET MILITARY MISSION IN ALASKA
MAY 1944 — SEPTEMBER 1945

COLONEL RUSSELL KEILLOR, BRIG. GEN. D. V. GAFFNEY,
CG ALASKAN DIVISION ATC, COLONEL KISILEV
SEPTEMBER 1944

RECEPTION FOR MAJ. GEN. IVAN A. OBRAZKOV

DECEMBER 1944

MRS. P. S.
COL. KEILLOR—
ANNIVERSARY

PARTY GIVEN BY SOVIET
PERSONAL TO COM-
MEMORATE THE SECOND
YEAR OF FERRYING
ACTIVITIES ON THE
ALSIB ROUTE.

THE RUSSIANS DEPART SEPTEMBER 1945

Russian personnel who participated in the Lend-Lease program, 1942-1945.   USAF

53

The track of the White Pass and Yukon Railway, laid down Broadway Street in Skagway during the Gold Rush heyday of 1898-1900, came to life again during World War II.
AHL

TRANSPORTATION SYSTEMS
BY LAND, WATER AND AIR

A look at a prewar map of Alaska and northwestern Canada shows few man-made transportation systems. The White Pass and Yukon Route connected tidewater at Skagway to Whitehorse, Yukon, and the Alaska Railroad connected tidewater at Seward to Fairbanks in interior Alaska. Valdez and Fairbanks were connected by the 360-mile Richardson Highway. A few short-run railroads and short stretches of gravel road were all that served the populated portions of Alaska.

The Northern Alberta Railroad, started in 1914 as a way to colonize the remote areas of Alberta and British Columbia, linked Edmonton to Waterways, Alberta, and Dawson Creek, British Columbia. Owned and operated jointly by the Canadian National and Canadian Pacific railroads, it had an undulating roadbed, laid over muskeg much of the way, and did not permit much speed or heavy loads. The Canadian National Railroad ran west from Edmonton to Prince George and Prince Rupert. Over these overtaxed routes, thousands of tons of war materiel had to pass from 1942 to 1944 to Dawson Creek, Prince Rupert and Waterways, the end of steel, for the two major construction projects--Alcan and Canol.

The other major transportation system that was just coming into its own before the war was the airplane.

Airplanes had been flown in the area since the early part of the century by pioneers such as C. H. Dickins, Capt. W. R. May, Walter Gilbert, Leigh Brintnell, Cy Becker, Noel Wien, Grant McConachie, Carl Ben Eielson, Joe Crosson, Harold Gillam, L. "Mac" McGee, Art Woodley and Bob Reeve.

The first flight in the North was in July 1913 at Fairbanks. A rapid development ensued, making Alaska the crossroads for northern or Great Circle routes to the Orient.

Many bush pilots and small companies flew into remote sites in Alaska and Canada, and large-scale commercial airline traffic was just beginning.

When war came to the North in June 1942 all commercial airlines in the area were placed under military orders and companies were ordered to fly all available aircraft to Edmonton for an important airlift operation to Fairbanks and Nome, Alaska.

All through the war the large and small airlines played an important part in ferrying men and supplies to the remote regions of the North.

THE WHITE PASS AND YUKON ROUTE

The Klondike Gold Rush in the Yukon in 1897 spawned a narrow-gauge railroad between Alaska and Canada that was to play an important part in the military buildup of the area.

S.S. Yukon, *an old Alaska Steamship Company ship was used to haul men and supplies to Alaska during the war.*

R.E. Schiller
Rockford, Illinois

Thousands of gold prospectors were swarming up the Inside Passage of Alaska in 1897, crossing the formidable coastal range passes--the Chilkoot and White--and floating down the Yukon River 500 miles to the gold fields in the Klondike River area near Dawson City, Yukon.

The need for a more efficient method of crossing the passes of the St. Elias Range from tidewater in Alaska to Lake Bennett in British Columbia became evident at the height of the Gold Rush in 1897. A group of British financiers decided to build a narrow-gauge railroad over the mountains. Construction began in 1898 and was completed two years later.

Through the years there were many lean times. The Gold Rush had ended by 1900, and the mining areas were being consolidated by large companies. By World War II, the railroad was in terrible condition. Although it could handle peacetime demands, it was overwhelmed by the material that poured into Skagway in 1942 for the Alaska Highway and Canol Project. Docks and railroad equipment alike were inadequate. Fewer than a dozen engines were in working order and the roadbed was desperately in need of repair.

So the railroad was leased to the U.S. Government for the duration of the war, and the U. S. Army took over its operation, retaining the civilian employees. The 770th Railway Operating Battalion of the Transportation Corps officially assumed control on October 1, 1942, and operated the road until the war was over. Most of the men in the battalion were from Southern states, and on their introduction to the North Country, they encountered one of the worst winters in its history.[1]

Rolling stock was built at the repair yards in Skagway and even one of the old locomotives that had run to the Klondike gold fields was put into service.

Locomotives were brought north from all over the country to supplement the aging ones still in service. In 1943, ten steam engines consigned to Iran were diverted to Skagway, converted from metered gauge to the three-foot narrow gauge and used for the rest of the war.

During the war the railroad accumulated 36 locomotives and almost 300 freight cars, some built for service in South America. More than 280,000 tons of materiel were carried to Whitehorse in 1943--45,000 tons in August alone. Thousands of troops and construction workers were also carried in both directions.

At the height of operations in 1943, dozens of trains rolled between Skagway and Whitehorse every day. As the war approached its end, the pressure eased, and none too soon. The railroad was literally worn out.

The 770th Railway Operating Battalion continued to run the railroad until control was returned to the pre-war management on May 1, 1946.

---

[1]The troops who took over the railroad during World War II faced some of the worst winters since the construction days of 1898-1900. Even with the help of bulldozers, the rotary snowplows could not keep up, and the line closed for 10 days in 1944. The temperature dropped so low that the engine wheels froze to the rails. Some of the rolling stock that had been sent north to help with the war traffic just was not suited to the extreme temperatures.

The Skagway dock in September 1942.   *USA*

The railroad at the White Pass summit on the border between Alaska and British Columbia in 1944.   USA

A rotary snowplow clears the track near White Pass in British Columbia in 1944.   USA

Troops bound for Whitehorse board the train at Skagway. The passenger cars were left over from the gold rush days 42 years before. USA

Whitehorse, Yukon, the headquarters for the Northwest Service Command, was one of the main supply points for the Alaska Highway and Canol Project. During the war the town grew from a population of 300 to more than 20,000. USA

Soldiers at the Skagway railroad yard. The locomotive is one of those built for service in Iran but redirected to the White Pass to help haul material to Whitehorse. *DP*

Troops of Company B, 770th Railway Operating Battalion, at Skagway in March 1944. *DP*

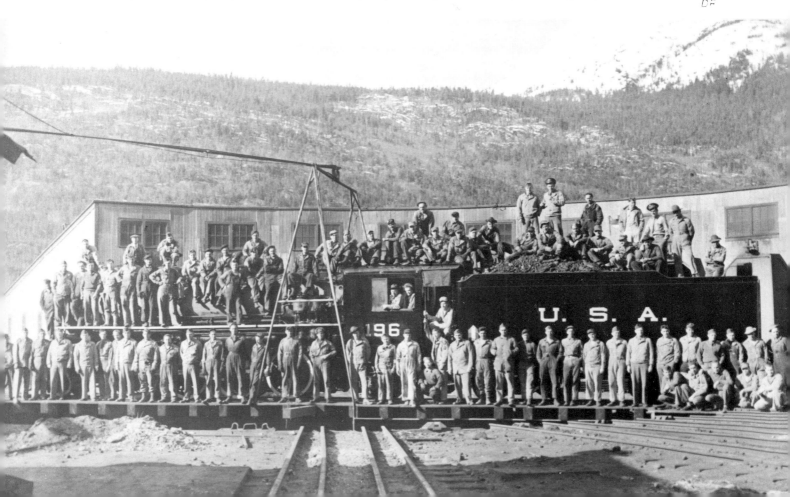

THE ALASKA RAILROAD

The other major land transportation system in the North was the Alaska Railroad. From the beginning of its operation in 1923, the railroad became the lifeblood of the Alaska interior.

In the early years of the century, Alaskans wanted an all-American, dependable, year-round transportation system that would lower shipping costs. Until that time, freight had to come over the White Pass and Yukon Route through Canadian territory and then down the Yukon River system by steamboat to Fairbanks, or by ocean steamer to the mouth of the Yukon River on the Bering Sea and then upriver by steamboat to Fairbanks. Both ways were expensive, time-consuming and for summer use only.

Coal was another factor in the proposal to construct a railroad. It would produce revenue to keep the road operating.

In 1912 President Taft authorized an Alaska Railroad Commission to survey the possibility of a route from tidewater at Seward on the Kenai Peninsula north to the site of Anchorage, through the Susitna River Valley to Mt. McKinley and Fairbanks. The line would stretch more than 470 miles and provide an all-weather route to the interior.

In 1914 President Wilson signed a railway bill that authorized construction and survey parties to go into the field in the spring. Several small existing railroad lines were bought along the route and construction began in 1915. It would take eight years to complete the line at a cost of $35 million.

Like so many others, the railroad had its ups and downs through the 1920s and 30s. The coming defense establishment and war years would tax it beyond its capabilities. The two main purposes of the railroad at the start of the war were to carry construction material, supplies and troops to Anchorage and Fairbanks and to keep military fuel tanks replenished with aviation gas for the airfields at Fairbanks and Nome.

Otto F. Ohlson took over management of the railroad in 1928 and held the job through the war years. He was a strong advocate for the re-routing of the road to Passage Canal, thus cutting out the hazardous winter route from Seward.[2]

[2]Otto Ohlson fought for years to get his Passage Canal route constructed. He wanted to close down the port at Seward and the railroad route between Seward and Portage. All civilian cargo would be transported through the new port of Whittier. Because of political considerations and the lack of material to construct a new town at Whittier during the war the Seward port and line north were never closed.

Passage Canal was on an arm of Prince William Sound southeast of Anchorage. By building what was to become known as the Alaska Railroad (or Whittier) Cut-off, the distance to Anchorage would be shortened by 54 miles. There would be an ice-free port at Whittier, freight rates would be reduced and the area would be farther away from possible enemy attack.

The Army had investigated the southern route from Seward to Anchorage in 1940 to determine whether it should rebuild the line from Seward north, build a port at Anchorage or build a new port at Passage Canal.

In April 1941, President Roosevelt signed an appropriation bill authorizing construction of the Cut-off project. Defense needs obliterated any thought of rebuilding the Seward-Anchorage line at this time. Seward's dock facilities could not handle the increased freight coming in for the new air bases under construction at Fairbanks and Anchorage plus other military and civilian projects.

In June 1941, the Corps of Engineers contracted with West Construction Company of Seattle to begin building the Cut-off route in the fall. After the alignment was established, two tunnels were blasted through the mountains at a narrow neck of the Kenai Peninsula to connect Whittier with Portage on the main line of the Alaska Railroad, 14.2 miles away. One tunnel was 13,005 feet long, the other 4,960 feet. They were completed in November 1942, and the Cut-off route was opened to traffic in June 1943. Built at a cost of $11 million, it was one of the largest railroad construction projects of the war in the North. It was operated by the Army throughout the war and served one of the most important ports in Alaska.

After Pearl Harbor, the railroad had trouble keeping enough manpower to run profitably and safely. Manpower shortages were also critical at the railroad's coal mine operation at Elsa. Soldiers had to be shifted to the mines to keep the road supplied with enough coal to run its trains.

Under the burden of the increased tonnage after 1940, the railroad was literally falling apart.[3] Because of pressing needs elsewhere, it did not have the manpower to rebuild the roadbed, or the material to do it. Hundreds of workers went into the Army or to better-paying jobs.

[3]Tonnage carried during the war years was as follows: 1939--157,900; 1940--194,400; 1941--361,000; 1942--419,800; 1943--461,400; 1944--627,800; 1945--549,200.

A call went out from the Alaska Defense Command in 1943 for help from the Army's Transportation Corps to keep the railroad operating. The 714th Railway Operating Battalion took over operation of the road on April 3, 1943, with 25 officers and 1,000 enlisted men. They had been training on the Chicago, Milwaukee, St. Paul and Pacific Railroad in the Northwest. They stayed on duty until May 1, 1945, and the last troops did not leave until that August. Thus both major railroads in the North were now operated by Army personnel.

This takeover helped considerably, but the battalion could never get enough experienced men to take care of everything. Because of bad track, derailments increased during the war years.

Equipment, some new and some used, was bought whenever it could be found. In June 1944 the first two diesel locomotives were bought for use on the Whittier run.

During the war many other railroad construction projects were carried on by the Army. A new dock was built at Seward, an ocean dock at Anchorage was reconstructed, a branch line was built to the new air base at Ladd Field near Fairbanks, and a bypass was built around the Loop district's wooden trestle on the Seward-Anchorage line.

Both railroads, although taxed far beyond their capacities during the war, played a vital part in the defense of Alaska and northwestern Canada.

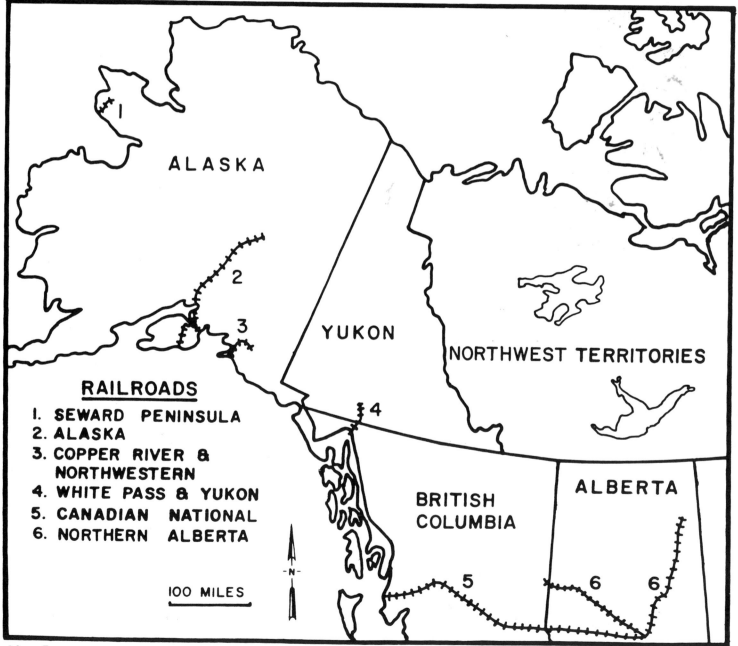

Map 5
Railroads of the North Country.

Troops visit a mobile post exchange. Most often a PX was a store in a fixed location, but that wasn't practical for troops assigned to duty along the 500 miles of the Alaska Railroad. A motor truck mounted on rails pulled a trailer which contained the counter for the PX.

USA
AHFAM
Alaska Railroad Collection

Barracks in the upper end of Whittier on Sept. 4, 1943.

Maj. Gen. S. B. Buckner and party prepare to set off a blast at the entrance to one of the two tunnels built for the Whittier Cut-off branch of the Alaska Railroad on Nov. 20, 1942.

General view of the Whittier area in June 1943.

AHFAM
Alaska Railroad Collection

OTHER RAILROAD OPERATIONS

Two other shortline railroads were operated by the Army during the war years in Alaska. The Copper River and Northwestern Railway ran between Cordova and Kennecott, a distance of 195 miles. The 713th Railway Operating Battalion operated an 11-mile section of this standard gauge road. Running northwest 86 miles from Nome to Shelton was the narrow-gauge Seward Peninsula Railroad. The Army rebuilt part of the line but due to the tundra conditions the roadbed sank into the soil every spring. A train was pulled by automobiles in the summer and dog teams in the winter, but despite this 100,000 tons were hauled during the Nome buildup in the winter of 1942.

One of the most unusual railroad operations of the war was the armored train that ran on the Canadian National tracks between Terrace and Prince Rupert, British Columbia. The Japanese had fished in the waters around Prince Rupert for years, and since the railroad from Terrace followed the Skeena River for 80 miles, it was feared that Japanese saboteurs might land and blow up a bridge or tunnel and block the vital rail line. An armored train was built in Winnipeg and delivered to Terrace in July 1942. It was composed of a flatcar with a 75-mm gun, searchlight and diesel operated generator, another car with two 45-mm Bofors guns, a steel coach carrying a platoon of infantry, a locomotive, a steel car serving as a train office and first aid station, another coach with two platoons and two additional cars with 75-mm and 45-mm guns.

The train made a trip each way every day between Terrace and Prince Rupert, but when the enemy threat subsided the train was discontinued.

TRANS-CANADIAN, ALASKA AND WESTERN RAILWAYS PROJECT

Some wartime construction proposals were not implemented. One of the largest was the Trans-Canadian, Alaska and Western Railroad, which was the subject of much study in 1942-43.

Frederic A. Delano, an uncle of President Roosevelt, an ex-railroad man and the president of the National Resources Planning Board in the President's Executive office, proposed the railroad project in March 1942.

It would traverse a route more than 2,000 miles long from Prince George, British Columbia, to a point on the Bering Sea on the west coast of Alaska, and would provide an additional transportation network for Russian lend-lease.

With an appropriation of $2.8 million the Army began a survey from Prince George, through the Rocky Mountain Trench to Watson Lake, Yukon, then west to Fairbanks. A route was also to be studied west from Fairbanks to a point near Teller on the Bering Sea on the Seward Peninsula. The Canadian government gave its approval.

The western survey from Fairbanks was to include a study of a possible port on Alaska's west coast and was to gather as much information as possible about the land between Fairbanks and the coast. Port Clarence at Teller was determined to be the best site for a deep-water port.

The western land survey was made in May 1942 by dog team, boat and airplane. Many routes were investigated. It was determined that a railroad or highway route to the coast, a distance of 600 to 800 miles, was feasible but would be very hard to build because of remoteness, weather and soil conditions. It was concluded that the Yukon River Valley to the west would provide the best route. Thus the river could be used as a supply route. Crossing the Yukon River would be a major obstacle. The most likely site for a bridge was at Rampart Rapids, where an island in the middle of the river could be used as a bridge support.

The route from Prince George to Fairbanks was almost 1,500 miles long and was surveyed in the summer of 1942. An air reconnaissance was made first. In July, 24 crews were conducting surveys, with more than 500 people involved. It was found feasible to build the line north from Prince George, which was on the main line of the Canadian National Railroad, to Fort Frances, Yukon and then west to a point 84 miles south of Fairbanks to a juncture with the Alaska Railroad. The Yukon River would be crossed at Five Finger Rapids near Carmacks, Yukon; this would mean a slight hindrance to sternwheelers on the river. The highest point on the route was at Sifton Pass, at 3,273 feet. It was estimated that more than 4.5 million ties would be needed for the roadbed. All could be cut along the route. Diesel engines were recommended over coal-burning engines to reduce the possibility of setting forest fires. It would take 400 days using 17,000 construction workers to complete the project at a cost of $111.8 million. This would include all the necessary railroad and support equipment needed.[1]

A more detailed survey of the western route was conducted in the winter of 1942-43 and planning

---

[1] Construction equipment included: 163,000 tons of 60-pound rails, 34,000 tons of camp supplies, 22,000 tons of fuel, hundreds of trucks, tractors, bulldozers, barges, airplanes and buildings, 1,400 miles of telephone lines and more than 70 bridges.

was started on the huge port facilities that would be needed at Port Clarence. This port facility would consist of concrete floating piers, buildings, railroad yards and fuel storage tanks. The total cost would be more than $20 million.

It would take 400 days and 7,500 construction workers to construct the western portion at a cost of more than $60 million. A pipeline was also proposed to stretch from Teller to Fairbanks at a cost of $11.5 million.

Fort Gibbon, an abandoned military post, at Tanana, west of Fairbanks, was picked as a possible site for a river-rail terminal for rerouting shipments on the Yukon River.

The cost of the entire project was estimated at more than $230 million. May 1943 was proposed for the start of construction, but because of the rapidly changing military situation in Alaska and the Pacific in 1943-44 the idea was dropped.

ROAD AND WATER ROUTES

Road systems in northwestern Canada were poor or nonexistent prior to World War II. In northern Alberta and British Columbia, a road of sorts ran from Edmonton to Dawson Creek and Peace River. A winter haul road stretched from Dawson Creek through Fort St. John to Fort Nelson, 300 miles north of Dawson Creek. The rest of the country was virtually roadless wilderness. The Yukon Territory had a winter sled trail that was passable to vehicles in the few short summer months from Whitehorse to Dawson City, a distance of over 350 miles.

In Alaska, the Alaska Road Commission was established in 1905 when there were fewer than a dozen passable wagon roads. The highway system of interior Alaska was a development of the trail routes over which the Indians, traders and prospectors traveled. There was a military trail from Valdez to Eagle, built between 1899 and 1901 and in part incorported into the new Richardson Highway between Valdez and Fairbanks in 1907. By 1910 wagons could make the entire journey, and in 1913 the first automobile reached Fairbanks from the coast.[5]

Several other roads were built in the 1920s and 30s. In 1941 an important link was established with constructioin of the Glenn Highway between Anchorage and the Richardson Highway.

---

[5] The Richardson Highway was named for Brig. Gen. Wilds P. Richardson, the appointed head of the Alaska Road Commission in 1905 and a well-known Alaska explorer-engineer. He commanded the American Expeditionary Force to North Russia in 1919 and retired from the Army in 1920. He died in 1929. Fort Richardson at Anchorage is named for him.

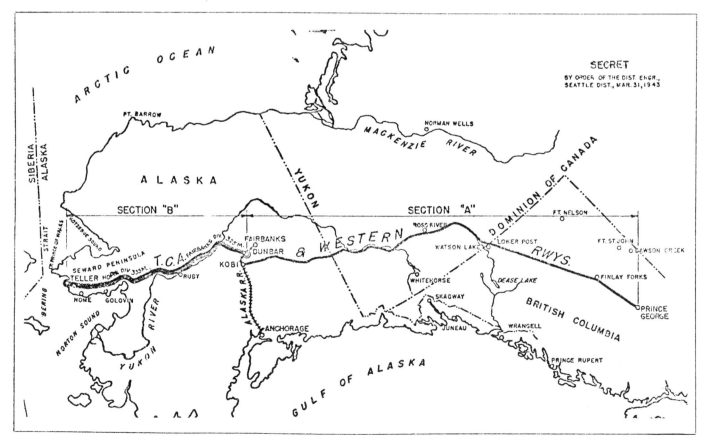

Map 6
Route of the proposed Trans-Canadian, Alaska and Western Railroad.   COE

Men of a Trans-Canadian Alaska and Western Railroad survey crew set up a "fly camp" near the Pelly River, Faro area, Yukon in 1942.   YA

To provide a shorter route to Valdez and Anchorage, the Slana-Tok Cut-off was built. The Skeena Highway, a 195-mile road between Prince George and Prince Rupert, was opened in September 1944 but was closed the first winter.

By the start of the war, however, the railroad and river routes along with expanded air service were still the most dependable means of transportation.

Major shipments of supplies were carried on the two great river systems of the North--the Yukon and the Mackenzie.

The Yukon flows from just above tidewater in southeast Alaska north and then west for more than 1,900 miles until it empties into the Bering Sea. Its major commercial tributaries are the Tanana, Porcupine, Teslin, Stewart and Pelly rivers.

From the Klondike Gold Rush to the end of the steamboat era in 1955, more than 250 boats plied the river, hauling supplies and passengers into the interior of Alaska and Yukon and hauling out the mineral production.

The Mackenzie flows north and west from Great Slave Lake to the Beaufort Sea, a part of the Arctic Ocean. With major tributaries--the Slave, Peace and Athabasca--it provides a 1,700-mile stretch of navigable water from Waterways, Alberta. It was the only surface route at the time to the Norman Wells oil field.

Since all major waterways freeze for seven to eight months a year, this form of transportation was good only for the short summer months. These river systems were especially important for the Canol construction project.

Even the ocean-going Princess ships of the Canadian Pacific Line were pressed into service. Prior to the war they had served the tourist trade in the Inside Passage between Vancouver and Alaska. The ships were painted battleship gray, and anti-aircraft guns were installed on board.

The **Princess Kathleen** and the **Marguerite** were reoutfitted and sent to the Mediterranean Sea for use as troop carriers. The **Marguerite** was sunk by a German U-boat on August 17, 1942.

A highway patrol stop on the Richardson Highway near Fairbanks in 1944.　　USA

Thousands of fuel drums rest on rafts for shipment on the Tanana River at Nenana, Alaska.　　USA

Equipment transported to Nenana, Alaska, via the Alaska Railroad is transferred onto a barge by a steam railway crane. The equipment will be pushed to Galena on the Yukon River by the sternwheeler Nenana. *USA*

An Army MT boat sits on a siding at Nenana, Alaska. They were shallow draft tugs used in rafting opertions on the Tanana River. *USA*

Aerial view of Whitehorse, Yukon in 1943. The edge of the airport is shown in the fore-ground.

Richard Finnie
Belvedere, California

TOWNS AND AIRFIELDS
FROM GHOST TOWN TO BOOM TOWN

DAWSON CREEK

Before 1942, Dawson Creek, British Columbia, was a hamlet of 300 to 400 people, the trade center for the Peace River country at the end of the rickety Northern Alberta Railroad. Beyond the town was a primitive dirt road to Fort St. John, 50 miles to the north, and beyond that, wilderness for hundreds of miles. Grain elevators were the most prominent structures in town.

With the start of construction of the Alaska Highway in the spring of 1942, thousands of troops and tons of equipment and supplies descended on the town. The population mushroomed by thousands. Streets were laid out in all directions and Nissen huts, tents and barracks sprouted on every corner. The limited town services could not begin to cope with this influx, and to make matters worse, the Canol Project the same year added its own infusion of men and material.

Dawson Creek had its "Halifax" situation, too, in February 1943.[1] A fire spread to an old livery stable where dynamite was stored. It blew up and the resulting fire destroyed the Dawson Hotel and an entire block of buildings.

FORT ST. JOHN

Fifty miles north of Dawson Creek lay Fort St. John, British Columbia. The original town was established 10 miles south of the present town on the Peace River in 1806. It was a trading post for the local Indians.

In 1941, it too was a small frontier town of 300, serving as a trading center for the area.

When the Northwest Staging Route airfield was built and the Alaska Highway construction crews came through in 1942, the town became a gigantic tent city of people. All existing buildings were taken over by the construction groups. Fort St. John became the southern sector headquarters for the highway construction project in 1942.

FORT NELSON

About 250 miles north of Fort St. John lay the town of Fort Nelson, British Columbia. It was connected to the south by a winter haul road that became impassable with the spring thaw.

The town was at the northern edge of the Peace River country on the Fort Nelson River, and had been established in the early 1800s as a fur trading post.

Besides being another site for a Northwest

Staging Route airfield, it was the focal point for highway construction both north and south. To the north was wilderness for more than 300 miles to Lower Post-Watson Lake. To the south was a most difficult stretch of highway to Fort St. John. A side road from here was also built north to Fort Simpson on the Mackenzie River in the Northwest Territories. This served as another access point for supplying the Canol Project.

WATSON LAKE

Just north of the old Hudson's Bay Trading Post of Lower Post, British Columbia, lay the village of Watson Lake, Yukon. It was halfway between Fort Nelson and Whitehorse. Another Northwest Staging Route airfield was built here.

During the Klondike Gold Rush, prospectors passed through the area on their way to the northern gold fields from the Stikine and Peace River systems.

Watson Lake, too, became an important construction site on the Alaska Highway.

WHITEHORSE

The Klondike Gold Rush led to the development of Whitehorse on a flat next to the Yukon River. World War II brought the town into the 20th century. Although continuing railroad and riverboat traffic had kept it from becoming a ghost town, its population by 1941 was only 650 in the summer and 350 in the winter.

At the beginning of the Alaska Highway construction, the town became the center for projects north toward Fairbanks and south to Watson Lake. Whitehorse was a little over halfway from Dawson Creek to Fairbanks. It provided good access to the highway from the White Pass and Yukon Railroad and the airport built above the townsite. It was picked as the headquarters for the entire construction project and the Northwest Service Command.

Oil from Norman Wells flowed in 1944 to a Whitehorse refinery that had been shipped north and reconstructed at the edge of town. The airport on the bluffs above town buzzed with the activity of Russian lend-lease and military flights to Alaska.

Whitehorse was a boom town in all respects. By 1943 more than 20,000 people were trying to live on a site that had accommodated only a few hundred in pre-war years.

Thousands of soldiers and construction workers passed through or were quartered here. In 1943 the town had only three beer taverns and three hotels--the Whitehorse Inn, the White Pass and

---

[1]In 1917, a French munitions ship exploded in the harbor of Halifax, Nova Scotia. The explosion wrecked a large part of the city and killed more than 1,600 people.

the Regina. Rooms were at a premium and those lacking priority status, which could mean many things to many people, could end up spending considerable time in hotel lobbies, if they were available. It got so bad that rooms on some of the riverboats were rented out when the boats were docked in town. Liquor was expensive and could be bought only by the sealed bottle at a government liquor store. Entertainment was spartan, especially in the dead of winter. In summer, the streets were alternately a dust bowl or a sea of mud, and the most popular sport was swatting mosquitoes. In winter, the temperatures sank as low as 50 degrees below zero.

As the war wound down, so did Whitehorse, but it would never again be just the end point for a small railroad and riverboat system.

EDMONTON

Edmonton was the center of military activity in northwestern Canada. It was the largest city in Alberta, with a pre-war population of 90,000. By 1942 its population had jumped to more than 120,000 and like other northern boom towns, it had a severe housing problem. The city was the crossroads for American soldiers and construction workers and Canadian airmen and workers headed for projects in the north.

As a trading post established on the Saskatchewan River in 1795, Edmonton served as a center of the fur trade in the Canadian North. When the province of Alberta was created in 1905, Edmonton was picked as its capital. Oil, coal and agriculture were the main industries of the region. Its municipal airport was an important center for all military and civilian flights to northern Canada and Alaska, including the Russian lend-lease planes. It was also an important railroad center. War materiel was shipped from here west to Prince Rupert and Dawson Creek and north to Waterways for the Canol Project.

The city was the true gateway to the North Country during the war and afterwards.

PRINCE RUPERT

One of the most important port facilities on the North Pacific coast was at Prince Rupert, British Columbia, just 90 miles south of Ketchikan, Alaska. When Canada went to war in September 1939, Canadian troops garrisoned the town, anti-aircraft guns were placed there and permanent camps were built.

With the consent of the Canadian government, Prince Rupert was activated as a sub-port of the Seattle Port of Embarkation on Feb. 20, 1942, to relieve the overtaxed ports of Seattle and San Francisco and provide a port closer to Alaska. Supplies and troops could be brought in over the Canadian National Railroad from Prince George and points south and east.

New dock facilities were built and others improved. A large U.S. Army camp was built on Acropolis Hill, a flat-topped hill overlooking the town. At Port Edward, 12 miles south of Prince Rupert, a camp was established to process troops going to areas of Alaska and the Pacific. More than 35,000 troops and civilians passed through the camp in a little over two years.

On both Kaien and Digby Islands forts were built to protect the city in case of an enemy attack. A submarine net was stretched across the harbor entrance between Casey Point and Kaien Island and Charles Point on Digby Island. The Canadian Navy and Air Force had establishments in the area and were in constant patrol for enemy submarines.

In three years of war more than 1.6 million tons of freight were transshipped through Prince Rupert to points in Alaska and the Pacific. The shipyard and drydock was a busy place during the war, building and repairing many types of ships, including several Russian ships in for complete overhauls.

From a prewar population of around 7,000, Prince Rupert boomed to more than 21,000, and the town lived on a war footing until late in 1944. At the end of the war the city simmered down to its pre-war population.

ANCHORAGE

Until 1915, the site of Anchorage on the Ship Creek flats was just marshy ground useful mainly for moose browsing. It was on Cook Inlet, named for Capt. James Cook, the British sea captain who stopped there in the late 1700s during his search for the Northwest Passage connecting the Atlantic and Pacific oceans.

In 1915 the Alaska Railroad Commission picked this place for a new permanent town built around the Alaska Railroad yards. Anchorage was to be laid out as an orderly town, in contrast to the helter-skelter arrangements of past mining boom towns in the Territory. The federal government would control the town during construction of the Alaska Railroad.

The orderly layout of Anchorage did not keep the normal frontier pastimes of drinking, gambling and prostitution from invading the area. It became a true "Wild West" town with some of the highest prices in Alaska.

Until 1940, Anchorage had a normal population of about 4,000, a lot by Alaska standards. The congressional appropriation for construction of Fort Richardson-Elmendorf Field on April 4, 1940, changed the town's character almost overnight.

In California a call went out for 1,000 workers to go north to work on construction projects. Men started streaming into Anchorage from all over the country. In late June 1940, 800 officers and men of the 4th Infantry Regiment arrived at Anchorage, the first trickle in what became a three-year flood of troops.

Anchorage took on a boom town atmosphere. Streets, even those that were paved, were dusty in summer, and most of the businesses along them were either bars or liquor stores.[2] This was in marked contrast to the major Canadian boom town of Whitehorse.

Anchorage became the headquarters for the Alaska Defense Command and continued its military importance until the latter part of 1944.

NOME

Situated on the southern coast of the Seward Peninsula, facing Norton Sound, Nome was another child of a gold rush. It was the largest town on the west coast of Alaska and was the site of a major air base built during the war. The only way to supply the site was by ship, for a few months each summer, and by air. Nome was also the final stop for Russian lend-lease planes before they were flown to Siberia.

In 1942 a massive sea and airlift was undertaken to Nome in response to fears of a Japanese invasion. The danger passed, but Nome remained an important military base.

SITKA

Sitka was the former capital and most historic town in Alaska. It was here in 1867 that the Stars and Stripes were raised over the land, ending Russia's presence in North America.

Sitka possessed a natural harbor, and in 1940 Congress authorized naval bases there and at Kodiak and Dutch Harbor. The base was built on Japonski Island across the bay from Sitka. Ironically the island was named by Baranof, the Russian founder of Sitka, because he was going to set up a concentration camp there for Japanese who might interfere with his ambitious plans to take over the whole North Pacific area.

---

[2]Joe E. Brown, well-known Hollywood star as he viewed Anchorage's 4th Avenue for the first time stated: "My what a large liquor store."

The **City of Baltimore,** an old ocean vessel was towed to Sitka from Chesapeake Bay and housed a thousand workmen working 10-hour shifts. More than $40 million was spent on the Naval Air Station and related facilities, including Forts Ray, Babcock, Peirce and Rousseau, during the war.

Although Sitka was never really threatened, it did have a scare right after Pearl Harbor. A whale, thought to be an enemy submarine, was destroyed by Navy scout planes, proving that they could hit a target.

SKAGWAY

Like Whitehorse and Dawson City, Skagway was born of the Klondike Gold Rush, but by World War II, its days of glory were since past. It was not a ghost town, however, for it was the southern terminus of the White Pass and Yukon Railroad and the gateway to the Yukon.

World War II transformed Skagway. It became a boom town again. The U.S. Army took over the railroad, and thousands of troops were quartered in town before being sent north to the Alaska Highway and Canol Project. The docks were not equipped to handle the flood of supplies, and although more docks were built, they were never adequate for the quantity of materials.

Skagway also became a strategic point for the transshipment of oil through a pipeline that paralleled the railroad right-of-way to Whitehorse.

JUNEAU

Juneau was the first major gold town in Alaska, the capital and largest city. It was an important stop on the Inside Passage route to Skagway. During the war its port facilities and airfield were modernized.

KODIAK

Before the war, Kodiak was a sleepy little fishing village on Kodiak Island. The island, largest in Alaska, measures 100 miles by 60 miles. It was settled by the Russians in 1792 and was famous for its bear population.

As war clouds gathered, Kodiak was selected as the site for the biggest of the three naval bases in Alaska because of its strategic position and its ability to harbor a fleet. At the site on Woman's Bay a huge naval base and army camp were under construction at the time of Pearl Harbor. Only a hangar and runways had been completed, and the garrison had only a 17-minute supply of ammunition on Dec. 7.

Fort Greely next to the naval base was being built at a cost of more than $17 million. Its primary mission was to guard the naval base. Fancy facilities were being built there and this had delayed construction before the war. A total of $75 million was eventually spent on the naval base, which served as an important headquarters during the Aleutian Islands campaign of 1942-43.

FAIRBANKS

Fairbanks began with the discovery of gold by Felix Pedro in 1902. It did not suffer the mushroom development that had plagued Dawson and Nome because gold-laden bedrock lay under 80 to 100 feet of mud and gravel. The lone miner working a small claim had no future in Fairbanks. Expensive mining machinery was required.

As the mining grew so did the town, and after the Alaska Railroad was completed in 1923, Fairbanks was truly the hub for all of interior Alaska.

In 1941 the city had 6,000 residents. During the war the population doubled. The city was directly linked to the outside world in May 1940 when American Airways inaugurated air service between Fairbanks and Seattle.

Military construction was started at Fairbanks in 1940. The installation was built as a cold-weather testing station, but it was soon named Ladd Field and became the northern terminus for the Russian lend-lease program.

With the completion of the Alaska Highway in 1943, Fairbanks was connected to the outside world by land and air, and, via the Alaska Railroad, by sea.

Yakutat, Alaska in 1943. It is between Juneau and Anchorage on the Gulf of Alaska.
NA

75

The main street of Dawson Creek, British Columbia, in January 1944.　　　*USA*

Dawson Creek was the center of the great Peace River wheat country and an important military outpost during the war.　　　*PAA*

In February 1943 the center of Dawson Creek was destroyed by a dynamite explosion and fire. These views show some of the damage.
Lloyd Wickliff.
Indianapolis, Indiana

Main Street, Fort St. John in August 1942. Like other towns on the Alaska Highway and the Northwest Staging Route it was no longer an isolated village but an important site for the defense of Alaska and northwestern Canada. GAI

Aerial view of Fort St. John, British Columbia. NA

Watson Lake, Yukon, located between Fort Nelson and Whitehorse on the Alaska Highway. A major airfield was also located here.   *USA*

Burwash Landing, Yukon on Kluane Lake. In years past this was a base for hunting parties going into the backcountry. It was a major construction base on the highway.
                                                                                                          NA

The Whitehorse waterfront in 1944.

USA

New hangar construction at the White Horse airport in October 1943. Parked on the apron for refueling are fighters and bombers bound for Russia.

Richard Finnie
Belvedere, California

The liquor store in Whitehorse during the war was probably the most popular business in town. *YA*

American troops stand at attention as Canadian troops march along Main Street in White-horse in 1943. The Canadians were leaving for the "outside." *USA*

View of the freight yards at the Prince Rupert Sub-port of Embarkation.

Phylis Bowman
Prince Rupert, B.C.

Aerial view of the large U.S. Army camp on Acropolis Hill above Prince Rupert, B.C.

Phylis Bowman
Prince Rupert, B.C.

Anchorage, Alaska in August 1940.   NA

An aerial mosaic of Fort Richardson and Elmendorf Field at Anchorage, Oct. 2, 1943.   AAC

-93 Sitka, Alaska

Sitka, Alaska, in 1940. This was before the seaplane base and harbor defenses were constructed. SC

Sitka in July 1941. Barracks have been built on Alice and Charcoal Islands and a seaplane base on Japonski Island. NA

Skagway, Alaska in 1945.

NA

The mayors of Juneau and Skagway, Alaska, and Alameda, California along with a Juneau councilman, inspect the preliminary work on an air raid shelter that was bored into the solid rocks of a mountainside for the protection of the residents of Juneau. It would have wooden floors and walls, running water, electric lights, kitchen, first aid section and sleeping quarters. Even Juneau was affected by the war scare that hit Alaska after Pearl Harbor.

NA

Barracks at the new post, Fort Greely, on Kodiak Island in December 1940.   NA

Kodiak Naval Base in July 1941.   The seaplane base and harbor are in the left fore-ground, the airstrip in the right background.   More barracks are shown in the left back-ground.
NA

Fairbanks, Alaska during the war. Founded in the early 1900s as a gold rush camp it grew along the Chena River to become the hub of interior Alaska, the northern terminus of the Alaska Railroad, the Alaska Highway, and the site of Ladd Field. NA

Waterfront view of Fairbanks in December 1943. USA

Street scenes of Fairbanks in 1944. First Avenue is on top, Cushman Street is on the bottom.
UAA

The army camp on Annette Island, built in 1940-41 under the Army's rapid defense expansion. Civilian Conservation Corps men were brought up from the States to work with Army engineers and the U.S. Forest Service. Permission was received from the Metlakatla Indian Community to build the base on the Island.   NA

The military airfield at Galena, Alaska on the Yukon River. This was an important stop on the air route from Fairbanks to Nome for the ALSIB program.   AAC

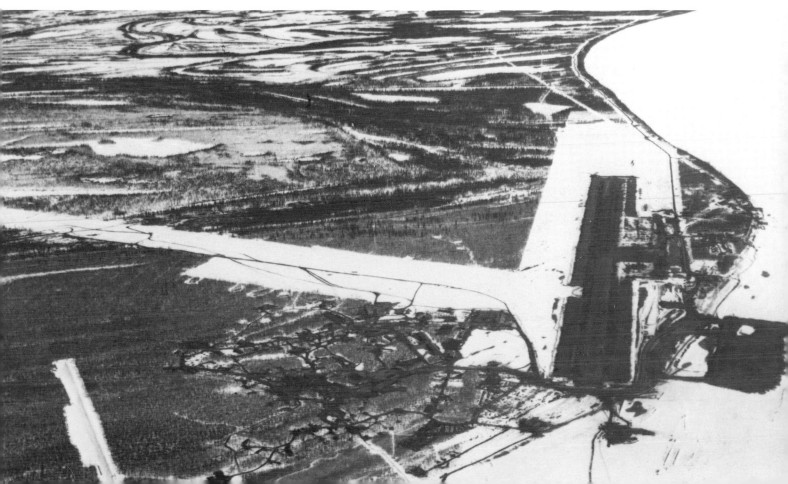

Fort Richardson was a tent city in 1940 when the first Alaska defense troops arrived. The fort was to become an important, permanent military installation.

FR

NORTH COUNTRY
AT WAR
TOO MUCH, TOO LATE

PACIFIC COAST MILITIA RANGERS

The western coast of Canada lay defenseless at the time of Pearl Harbor. Most regular Canadian forces were in Europe. There were no ground forces to perform routine patrol duty, much less to repel an enemy invasion.

A volunteer militia unit consisting mainly of World War I veterans was formed. They were to act as coast watchers, aircraft observers and assistants to the Royal Canadian Mounted Police in the control of enemy aliens. The new force was named the Pacific Coast Militia Rangers. Units were stationed on Vancouver Island and the Queen Charlotte Islands.[1]

Number 135 Company, Yukon Rangers, was organized in February 1943 at Dawson City, Yukon Territory. One hundred and fifty men were enlisted. They received partial uniforms (no hats or shoes), World War I rifles, four Sten guns and a captured German Maxim machine gun. They trained at the present Diamond Tooth Gertie's Gambling Hall in Dawson City, firing rifles and hearing lectures on compass use, map reading, map making and scouting.

At the end of the war the ranger units disbanded, but members were allowed to buy their Marlin 30-30 carbines for $5 each.

NAVAL PETROLEUM RESERVE #4

Naval Petroleum Reserve #4 had been established on the Arctic Coast of Alaska around Point Barrow on Feb. 27, 1923. The 35,000-square-mile preserve was set aside for possible naval use in wartime.

The Bureau of Yards and Docks, under direction of the secretary of the navy, sent several reconnaissance parties to the area in March and June 1944 to determine the feasibility of establishing an oil drilling site for future oil prospecting.

On July 19, 1944, Seabee Detachment 1058, consisting of 181 men and 5 officers, left Tacoma, Washington, on two ships with 8,200 long tons of freight, enough to maintain operations for one year. PBYs flew along the route to Point Barrow and Cape Simpson to serve as lookouts for dangerous ice floes.

The detachment landed at Barrow in August and began construction of a camp and airstrip. The Naval Air Transport Service would serve the operation. Tractor-train convoys would then haul drilling supplies to the selected test drilling site at Umiat, on the Colville River, more than 330 miles from Barrow.

Because of the nature of the terrain, only a winter trip over ice and snow could be made to Umiat. This was undertaken in January 1945. The tractor-train consisted of four tractors with a bulldozer in front and 20 bobsleds behind. Travel continued around the clock. Wannigans, or house sleds, provided living quarters, radio stations, mess shacks, machine shops and storehouses. Dog sleds and snow jeeps broke trail, and aerial reconnaissance was started. There was constant radio contact with Barrow. By June, thousands of tons of materials had been hauled to the drilling site in three trips.

An airstrip was constructed and a test well drilled to 1,816 feet in the summer of 1945. Geologic investigations were conducted over the area during 1945 to gain some idea of the oil potential of the reserve.

At the end of the war, the Seabee unit was inactivated and all work was turned over to civilian contractors.

Capt. Charles Chapman of #135 Company, Yukon Rangers, at Dawson City, Yukon. Charles Chapman Watson Lake, Yukon

---

[1]*Its peak strength was in August 1943 when 14,849 men were organized into 115 companies.*

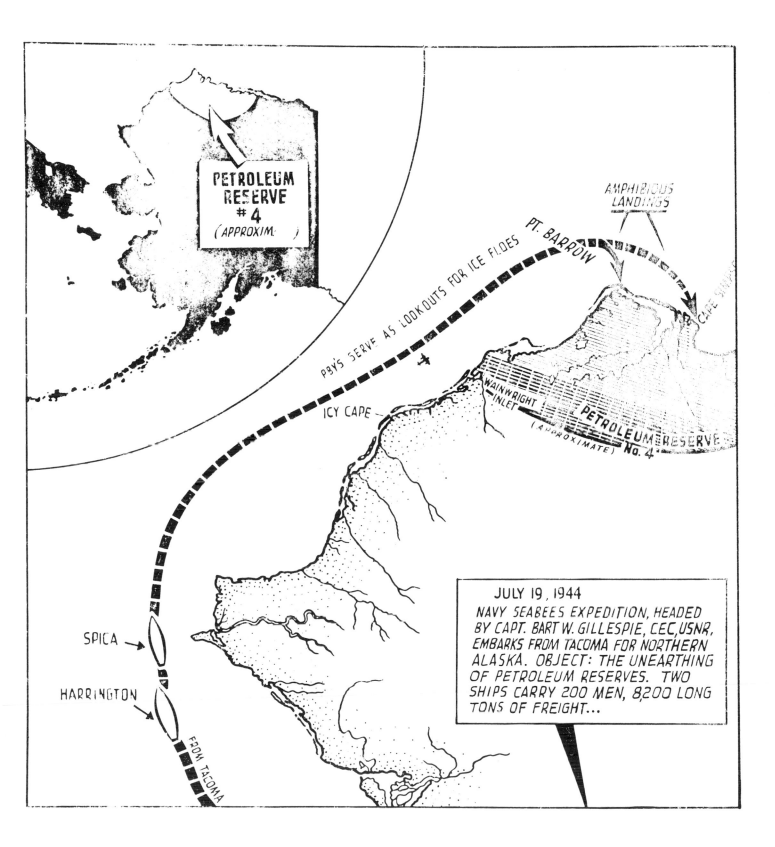

PETROLEUM
RESERVE
#4
(APPROXIM.)

PBY'S SERVE AS LOOKOUTS FOR ICE FLOES

PT. BARROW

AMPHIBIOUS
LANDINGS

ICY CAPE

WAINWRIGHT
INLET

PETROLEUM RESERVE
(APPROXIMATE) No. 4

SPICA

HARRINGTON

FROM TACOMA

JULY 19, 1944
NAVY SEABEES EXPEDITION, HEADED
BY CAPT. BART W. GILLESPIE, CEC, USNR,
EMBARKS FROM TACOMA FOR NORTHERN
ALASKA. OBJECT: THE UNEARTHING
OF PETROLEUM RESERVES. TWO
SHIPS CARRY 200 MEN, 8,200 LONG
TONS OF FREIGHT...

Map 7
Route of the Navy Seabee Expedition to the Arctic Slope in 1944.   NA

JAPANESE OPERATIONS

Japanese forces made several intrusions into Alaskan-Canadian territory between 1942 and 1945, including their large-scale invasion of Attu and Kiska and bombing of Dutch Harbor in June 1942.

At the time of Pearl Harbor, the 13th Naval District (Washington, Oregon and Alaska) had five World War I destroyers and 12 PBYs (6 in Alaska) for submarine patrol duty along the coast of British Columbia and Alaska. The Army Air Force had 61 pursuit planes and 86 medium bombers in the area for protection of the coast. Nine enemy submarines were reportedly sent to patrol off the North American west coast after Pearl Harbor.

On June 20, 1942, a Japanese submarine bombarded Vancouver Island at a lighthouse and radio station off Estevan Point, midway up the west coast of the island. This was the first and only attack of Canadian soil by a foreign power since formation of the country in 1867. The next day an enemy submarine attacked Fort Stevens at the mouth of the Columbia River. The sub fired 17 shells. This was one of the first attacks on the continental United States since the war of 1812.[2]

On the night of July 9, 1942, it was reported that an enemy submarine had been sunk off Annette Island in Southeastern Alaska by RCAF planes, the Coast Guard cutter **McLane** and a Coast Guard plane.

In 1944-45 the Japanese launched 9,300 paper balloons from northern Honshu Island. They carried 25 to 65 pounds of incendiary and anti-personnel bombs. It was hoped that the winds would carry these balloons to the timbered regions of the northwest, where they would fall and start forest fires. Between November 1944 and August 1945, 90 balloons, measuring 33 feet in diameter, were recovered from areas as far east as Michigan, in Mexico, Canada, Hawaii and Alaska. In Oregon in May 1945, one bomb-filled balloon killed six people when they tried to take it apart.

RUSSIAN RETURN TO ALASKA

A top-secret base for the training of Russian soldiers was established at Cold Bay after V-E Day in 1945. The Russians used landing craft to train in amphibious operations, supposedly for an entry into the war against Japan and a joint

[2]On Feb. 23, 1943, a Japanese submarine shelled Goleta, a few miles west of Santa Barbara, California, causing very minor damage. This was the first attack on American soil.

A Japanese balloon carrying bombs toward the Aleutians is shot down off Attu Island on Feb. 25, 1945. *USAF*

A fuse timing device from a Japanese balloon recovered eight miles west of Holy Cross, Alaska, on Jan. 21, 1945. *USA*

94

Russian-American invasion of the Kurile Islands. These plans were canceled when the war ended in August 1945.

ALASKA COMMUNICATIONS SYSTEM (ACS)

Communication among Alaskan military posts was a priority item in Alaska 80 years ago. In 1900, the Washington-Alaska Military Cable and Telegraph System, or WAMCATS, was established under U.S. Army Signal Corps direction. Gen. Adolphus Greely was in charge of this system and by 1903, military posts from the Bering Sea to Eagle to Valdez were in touch with each other and the outside world by land line telegraph and undersea cable.

In 1907, the first wireless (radio) system was established and through the years up to World War II, the land lines were slowly replaced by radio communications. The WAMCATS name was officially changed in 1936 to the Alaska Communications System (ACS).

The ACS was upgraded as defense spending increased before the war. Just after Pearl Harbor, certain commercial radio-telephone circuits between Alaska and Seattle were taken over by the military. Censorship was imposed and cryptography was put in use throughout the ACS.

The ACS was vastly expanded during the war. Part of the Alaska Railroad and Civil Aeronautics Authority communication systems were integrated with it. Two thousand troops were working on communications systems throughout Alaska and northwestern Canada during the war. During the Aleutian campaign, these troops performed valuable service providing radio and radar networks throughout the chain. They set up communication stations on every island occupied by Allied Forces.

During construction of the Alaska Highway and the Canol Project in 1942-44, radio and telephone service was provided by the ACS. On the highway, ACS personnel built more than 2,000 miles of telephone line using 72,000 poles. Telephone service was established between Fairbanks, Norman Wells and Edmonton and into the lower 48 states.

As the war wound down, the ACS like other defense esstablishments relaxed its complete military control and some of its services were once again open to civilian use in July 1944.

ALASKA TERRITORIAL GUARD

Gov. Gruening had pressured the War Department for authority to organize an Alaskan National Guard, but he had no success until mid-1940. Then the 297th Infantry Battalion was organized with companies in Ketchikan, Juneau, Anchorage and Fairbanks. It was called to active service on Sept. 15, 1941, leaving the Territory without any local defense force for a considerable time.

Vast areas of the Alaskan interior and coastline were exposed to possible Japanese attack at the start of the war, so Gruening again called for a homegrown military unit to act as coast watchers, aid the armed forces in rescue missions, and give whatever help it could in case of enemy attack.

Along with Capt. Carl Scheibner, the Governor's military aide, and Maj. Marvin "Muktuk" Marston, Gruening criss-crossed the state signing up over 3,000 Eskimos, Indians and Aleuts to his new "Tundra Army." The natives were united as never before and eventually the Alaska Territorial Guard, as it was known, had a total of 20,000 members, including women and children.

Marston commanded the western and central

A painting shows Maj. Marvin "Muktuk" Marston, the head of the western segment of the Alaska Territorial Guard, instructing one of his "Eskimo Scouts" in the use of a rifle.   AAC

The Alaska Territorial Guard marches toward the old Russian Orthodox Church in Sitka, Alaska.   UAA

Alaska Territorial Guards training at Point Hope in 1943.   FR

Alaskan communities, with the first unit established on St. Lawrence Island. Scheibner commanded eastern and southern Alaska units.

Most native members were either too old or too young for the draft or were deferred for family reasons. They served at their homes, received Enfield rifles and conducted military drills.

Maj. Marston became something of a legend during this period and was well-known to most of the natives in his Guard territory. He traveled from village to village by any means possible, checking on his men. Although the ATG never saw hostile action, it did perform some vital missions for the military and the unit was not disbanded until almost two years after the war.

ALASKA SCOUTS

Among the several small military units that were stationed in Alaska were the Alaska Territorial Guard, the 1st Special Service Force and the Alaska Scouts. The Scouts were also known as Castner's Scouts and Castner's Cutthroats. Formally they were the Alaska Combat Intelligence Platoon formed in November 1941 by Col. Lawrence V. Castner with Col. William Verbeck as second in command.

Castner was an intelligence officer for the Alaska Defense Command and had convinced Gen. Buckner that an independent intelligence-gathering unit would be needed in an area the size of Alaska.

The unit was composed of highly trained men who could land on enemy terrain, gather intelligence and return to their base. Many types were enlisted, including regular Army men, Aleuts, Indians, Eskimos, fox-trappers, prospectors and fishermen. They were all experienced in living off the land and handling themselves wherever they were stationed. They did not operate in platoon strength but were scattered throughout the Territory especially in the Aleutian area.

Castner's father, Joseph C. Castner, had formed the Philippine Scouts 40 years before as a similar organization. The Alaska Scouts took part in several military operations during the Aleutian campaign.

Castner and 37 of his men slipped into Adak on Aug. 28, 1942, and spent two days checking the island for possible Japanese occupation. They also were the first troops ashore during the Amchitka occupation on Jan. 12, 1943, and participated in the Attu invasion. One non-military operation was the evacuation of the native population of the Aleutian and Pribilof Islands to resettlement camps on Admiralty Island in southeastern Alaska.

Col. Lawrence V. Castner, commander of the Alaska Scouts. *USA*

NOME AIRLIFT

War jitters hit Alaska hard after the bombing of Dutch Harbor in June 1942. The enemy had occupied several western Aleutian Islands and there was a real possibility that a Japanese Naval Force was operating somewhere in the North Pacific-Bering Sea area. An intercepted Japanese message at Pearl Harbor indicated the enemy might be planning an invasion at Nome, although the U.S. Navy, through air and sea patrols, could find no sign of the enemy force.

"Operation Bingo," a massive airlift, was ordered by Gen. Buckner to bring in supplies for the defense of Nome. Buckner commandeered more than 40 commercial airliners that had gathered at Edmonton, and ordered them to fly his supplies 600 miles from Anchorage to Nome. In 36 hours, the planes had flown in more than 2,000 men to garrison the town and airfield and tons of war materiel. The airlift eventually brought in almost one half million tons of equipment, anti-aircraft guns and supplies.

By July 4 the scare and airlift were over, but excellent lessons had been learned from this massive movement of men and equipment by air.

The Pribilof Islands south of Nome were staffed by Signal Corps men who were to report any enemy sightings by radio. Although there were no enemy in the area, the men had to stay on the isolated island until October.

Nome was firmly established as an important air base for Russian lend-lease planes for the rest of the war.

EXCURSION INLET

Seventy miles northwest of Juneau is Excursion Inlet, an old Indian fishing village, that was picked to be the site of a large staging base for the upcoming Attu invasion. Gen. John DeWitt, Commander of the Western Defense Command, had ordered its construction over objections of Gov. Gruening, who thought that the existing facilities at Juneau would have served the purpose.

Major facilities which were built mainly by civilian contractors with units of the 331st Engineers were dry stores and subsistence warehouses, docks at storage areas, light ship repair facilities and an ammo dock located near the head of the bay. A hospital was located approximately two miles inland from the main area. A petroleum storage farm was literally imbedded in solid rock near the mouth of the bay.

The base was not finished in time for the Attu campaign, but DeWitt ordered it completed anyway. It was ready in late 1944, and from August through November 1945, German prisoners-of-war of the 1933rd Service Command Unit, Prisoners of War Camp demolished the port of embarkation.

"When the staging base at Excursion Inlet was conceived, our military intelligence was not accurately informed of the enemies strength or his long term objectives. Also, we must recognize that cost plus construction can not be terminated or interrupted in a hasty fashion. Should our resistance have been less than what we were able to afford, I am sure the enemy advance would have intensified. This base may have well served its purpose. Also, I feel that it was not in the initial conception that this base should be located at or near an inhabited civilian city (Juneau)."
R. E. Schiller
Rockford, Illinois

LOGGING, FOREST AND MINING ACTIVITIES

During the war the U.S. Government was running short of spruce lumber and was faced with going into the national parks for trees to supplement production from federal and private forests for aircraft production.

The National Park Service pointed out that much of the fine Sitka spruce in Alaska was going to waste and could be used. As a result, the Secretary of Agriculture approved an agreement between the Commodity Credit Corporation and the U.S. Forest Service under which the Alaska Spruce Log Program began producing logs for aircraft lumber from areas in the Tongass National Forest.

The Commodity Credit Corporation made available a revolving fund of $3.5 million to cover field operations. The corporation bought stumpage from the Forest Service, after which the program officers contracted the work to independent logging companies. The logs were assembled into rafts of about one million feet each and towed to Puget Sound, where they were offered for sale to mills specializing in cutting spruce airplane stock.

The lower grade logs were sawed by the Alaska mills, large quantities of this lumber being shipped to the Aleutians. The program was liquidated in the fall of 1944.

Serious forest fire losses had occurred in interior Alaska for many years. In 1939, an Alaskan Fire Control Service was organized under the General Land Office. In 1942, as a result of the war, the Fire Control Service was granted some of the emergency funds appropriated by Congress for protection of the forests and strategic facilities of the United States. This additional fund was continued through June 1945. They were able to establish a skeleton force of year-long personnel and supplement fire season fire guards.

Due to increased guard and wet summers, total burned acreages went from 4.5 million acres in 1940 to 117,000 in 1945.

In the search for strategic and critical minerals, engineers and geologists surveyed Alaska's great mineral wealth on a wider scale than ever before. They went into unexplored regions to seek ores vital to the war effort with the result that many new projects were opened in the three-year period in which gold mining was suspended. On June 30, 1945, the ban on gold mining was lifted.

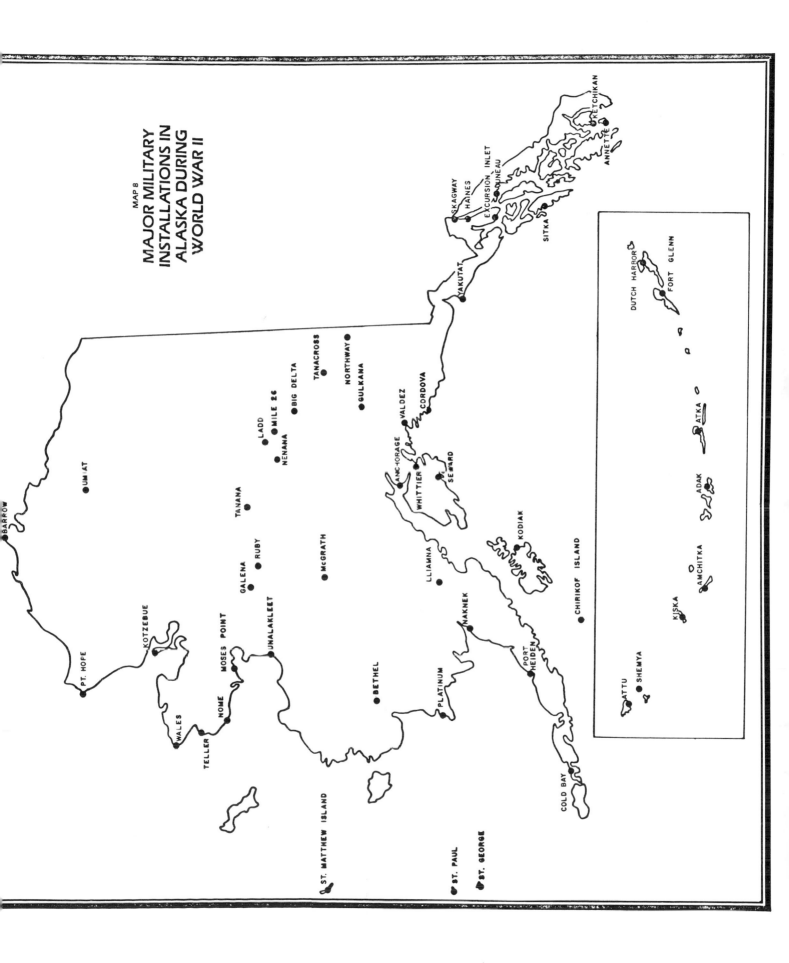

MAP 8

MAJOR MILITARY
INSTALLATIONS IN
ALASKA DURING
WORLD WAR II

BARROW

UMIAT

PT. HOPE

KOTZEBUE

WALES
TELLER
NOME
MOSES POINT
UNALAKLEET

GALENA
RUBY
TANANA

McGRATH

BETHEL

PLATINUM

ST. MATTHEW ISLAND

ST. PAUL
ST. GEORGE

LADD
NENANA
MILE 26
BIG DELTA

TANACROSS
NORTHWAY
GULKANA

ANCHORAGE
VALDEZ
CORDOVA
WHITTIER
SEWARD

LLIAMNA

NAKNEK

PORT
HEIDEN

COLD BAY

KODIAK

CHIRIKOF ISLAND

YAKUTAT

SKAGWAY
HAINES
EXCURSION INLET
JUNEAU

SITKA

KETCHIKAN
ANNETTE

DUTCH HARBOR
FORT GLENN

ATKA

ADAK

AMCHITKA

KISKA

ATTU
SHEMYA

EXCURSION INLET

The abandoned Indian village at the base site.

The abandoned cannery at the inlet.

ASTORIA & PUGET SOUND CANNING Co
LIC No 43-308 TRAP No 6

Docks and warehouse area at Excursion Inlet.

These floating barracks (wanigans) housed the advanced elements of the civilian construction force.

All photos from
R.E. Schiller
Rockford, Illinois

Troops on review. The large building behind was one of 20 permanent storage warehouses.

"E" Company's sawmill operation at the head of the inlet. Lumber was used for constructing the large buildings at the base.

This was the first large bridge constructed by the 331st Engineers. It led to the tank farm.

All photos from
R.E. Schiller
Rockford, Illinois

Several minerals from Alaska were very important to the war effort. Platinum was mined at Goodnews Bay north of Bristol Bay. Tungsten ore was developed along with mercury from deposits on the northern flanks of the Alaska Range.

A large deposit of jade, used in bearings for airplanes, was discovered in the Shungnak area of the Arctic. Also found in the area was a large quantity of tremolite asbestos, used as a filtering agent for blood plasma. The supply in the United States was almost exhausted at the time of the discovery.

Camp area at Fort Randall, Cold Bay in July 1942.   *USA*

Cold Bay with the new secret air strip in the background in May 1942.   *RC*

Comedian Joe E. Brown is flanked on the left by Lt. Com. James Russell and on the right by Col. Charles Corlett, garrison commander at Kodiak.

The Duke of Kent visits the Air Observers School in Edmonton, Alberta, in August 1941.

PAA

A williwaw (very strong wind that blows in all directions) lifting the water in Womens Bay at Kodiak Island.
RC

A group of United States senators, including Burton of Ohio, Holman of Oregon, Walgreen of Washington and Chandler of Kentucky, meet with Brig. Gen. Jesse Ladd and other officers in Alaska in August 1942.
USA

Movie star Ingrid Bergman visits the Fort Richardson hospital in 1943.

Jane Geitner Tucker
Old Tappan, N.J.

Marguerite Huron, an American Red Cross recreation worker, distributes presents at the Fort Richardson hospital, Christmas 1943.

Jane Geitner Tucker
Old Tappan, N.J

A Navy craft takes supplies to the natives of the Pribilof Islands.

UAA

Dog teams at an outpost in Alaska. The Army Quartermaster Corps used them to haul food to snowbound infantry units and to find and aid airmen forced down in the wilderness.

USA

Troops enroute to Alaska are issued Arctic equipment inside the Quartermaster Clothing Warehouse at the Prince Rupert Staging Area, Port Edward, B. C. in November 1944.

Troops enroute to Alaska check their equipment in their barracks at the Prince Rupert Staging Area, Port Edward, B.C. in November 1944.

Phylis Bowman
Prince Rupert, B.C.

One of the more than 40 volcanoes in the Aleutian chain.

Donald McKay
Little Rock, Arkansas

ALEUTIAN ISLANDS DEFENSES

A WOMAN BEHIND EVERY TREE

Boxes marked for the Blair Fish Packing Company, Umnak, Alaska, sat on the Seattle dock in late 1941 and early 1942. They contained war materiel destined for a secret airbase under construction with Gen. Buckner's blessing on Umnak Island in the eastern Aleutian chain. Civilian workers had also landed at Cold Bay on the Alaska Peninsula in August 1941 and unloaded boxes marked for Saxton and Company. This was supposed to be a fish cannery operation, but was in fact another secret airbase. These two bases, ready when the Japanese attacked Dutch Harbor on June 3-4, 1942, helped thwart a possible takeover of the naval station. The war in Alaska took a new turn after Dutch Harbor.

The Aleutian Islands, which are a partly submerged extension of the mountain chain that forms the Alaska Peninsula, stretch 1,100 miles from the tip of the Peninsula west to Attu. The Russian Komandorskis (Commander) Islands extend the chain another 300 miles to the west. The chain is made up of 279 islands ranging in size from Unimak, 70 miles by 20 miles, to

Soldiers' clothing testifies to the incessant cold.   NA

dozens of mere specks on the map. They are divided into six distinct island regions: the Fox, Delarofs, Islands of the Four Mountains, Andreanof, Rat and Near islands.[1] The maximum elevation is 9,372 feet. Forty-six volcanos dot the islands.

Because of the Japanese Current, the waters of the Bering Sea on the north side and the Pacific Ocean on the south are ice free.

Weather conditions are among the worst in the world. Violent winds (williwaws) blow daily along with fog, rain and snow. Measurable precipitation occurs on an average of 200 days a year. Temperatures are not as cold as in interior Alaska, seldom going below zero. Snow depths average one to two feet with occasional blizzards piling the snow up to six feet.

The topography is extremely rugged due to their volcanic origins on most of the islands. Glaciers and permanent snowdrifts dot the higher elevations.

In 1741, Vitus Bering sailed from the Siberian coast to discover Alaska for Czarist Russia. Soon, ruthless Russian frontiersmen roamed through the islands in quest of the lustrous pelts of the sea otter. The Russians used the stone-age natives, the Aleuts, as servants and eventually reduced their population by many thousands. The sea-otter herds were greatly diminished by ruthless hunting. Reduction of this resource helped Russia decide to sell its North American territory to the United States in 1867. The Aleutian Islands, along with most of Alaska, sank into obscurity for the next few decades.

The islands did not go unnoticed by the Japanese, however. In the early 1930s, the Japanese had largely depleted the run of fish off their own shore, and had begun to work off the coast of America, from Mexico to Alaska. In 1932 they sent floating canneries across the Bering Sea and subsequently extended their trips into Alaska's Bristol Bay region. In 1937, the U.S. State Department protested to Tokyo about Japanese encroachment on the fishing areas. The Japanese had also been examining the Aleutian Islands for years, and had even landed on some of them to take readings and draw maps. They had landed on St. Lawrence Island in 1937 and tried to barter liquor for fur boots. Submarine sightings had been reported off several islands.

From Attu in the far western part of the chain it is only 720 miles across the water to the

[1]The Shumagin and Sanak islands off the Alaska Peninsula are usually included with the Aleutian chain.

110

northern Kurile Islands of Japan and only 600 miles to the Soviet base at Petropavlovsk. So the islands were a gateway to Japan or to Alaska and the North American west coast.

By 1941 the stage had been set for a protracted war for these volcanic remnants. The fighting would take several thousand Japanese lives and hundreds of Allied lives and cost millions of dollars and tie up thousands of Allied troops in the area for almost two years.

Native villages existed on Akutan, Atka, Attu, Umnak, Unimak and Unalaska islands before the war. After the Japanese attack on Dutch Harbor, the native Aleuts were forced to evacuate their villages and were shipped to southeastern Alaska. Half of them never saw their homes again.

On June 16, 1942, the military transport **U.S.S. Delaroff** arrived at St. Paul Island, one of the Pribilof Islands north of the Aleutians, and evacuated residents to southeastern Alaska. Fourteen died on Admiralty Island before the others returned home in May 1944.

St. Paul Island was established as a LORAN (Long Range Aids to Navigation) station. Nine soldiers were stationed on this lonely island. They mined all the buildings in the village on the chance that the Japanese would invade.

When Buckner became commander of the Alaska Defense Force in 1940 he realized the importance of the Aleutians immediately. A survey of the islands in late 1940 was made and airfield sites were picked up and down the chain.

On March 3, 1942, the first plane landed on the completed runway at Umnak. The war machine had been brought to the islands.

President Roosevelt on his first tour of the Aleutians from Aug. 3 to 11, 1944, eats in a quonset hut on Adak.

NA

A Quonset hut takes form. The Quonset was one of the most popular and easiest buildings to erect. It was usually placed in a depression in the ground, with the excavated earth banked around it as a protection against bombs. They could be from 10 to 100 feet long, 16 feet wide and about 12 feet high at the center.   USA

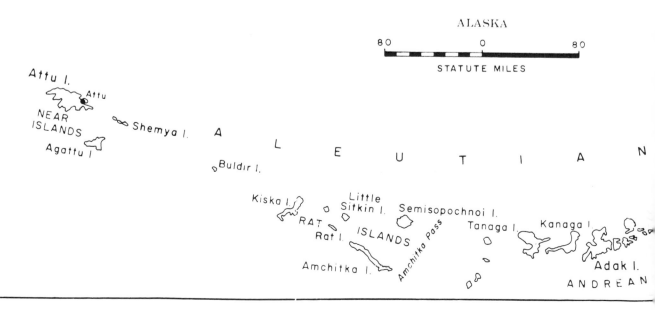

Map 9

ALEUTIAN ISLANDS

ALASKA

80   0   80

STATUTE MILES

Attu I.

Attu

NEAR
ISLANDS   ⚬⚬⚬ Shemya I.

Agattu I.

⚬Buldir I.

A   L   E   U   T   I   A   N

Kiska I.

RAT

Rat I.   ISLANDS

Amchitka I.

Little
Sitkin I.

Semisopochnoi I.

Amchitka Pass

Tanaga I.   Kanaga I.

Adak I.

ANDREAN

Evacuees from an Aleutian island stand on deck. Entire populations were removed from several Islands after the Japanese invasion. The principal victims were the Aleuts, close relatives of the Eskimos, who for countless centuries had eeked out a living by fishing and hunting in the Aleutians and other islands in the Bering Sea area.   NA

A typical post exchange in the middle of the boggy tundra on an Aleutian island.   *USAF*

Troops at Dutch Harbor look at pictures of movie stars.   *NA*

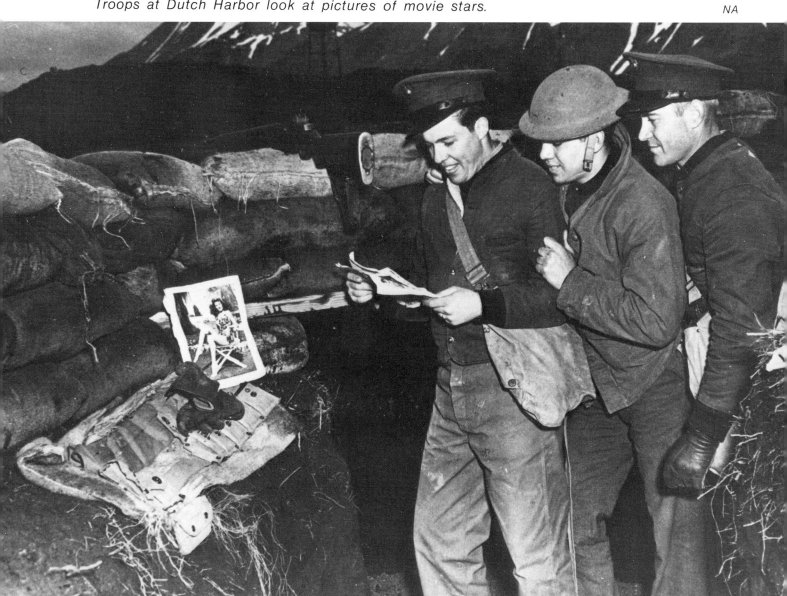

A Japanese prisoner is interviewed at Dutch Harbor in September 1942. He may have been one of the five enemy sailors captured when their submarine was sunk near Atka by two PBYs.   *NA*

Troops take a chow break while setting up camp after a dirty and wet landing on an Aleutian island.   *USA*

Movie Actress Olivia DeHaviland visits Col. Walter Hodge's headquarters at Fort Randall, Cold Bay, in 1944.

Reeve Collection

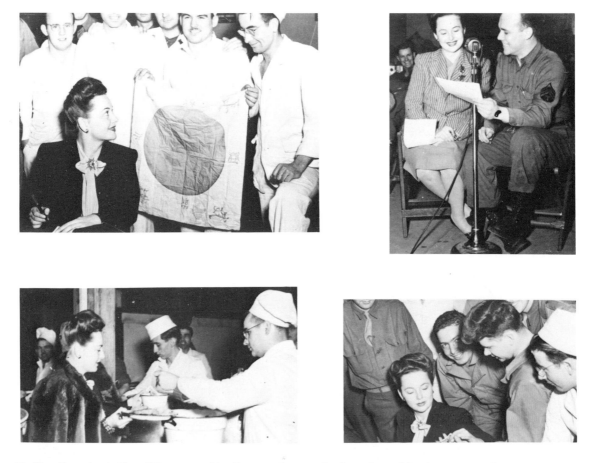

Olivia DeHaviland at the Shemya Air Force Base during her Alaskan tour in 1944.   *USAF*

Gov. Gruening arrives to inspect Shemya Air Force Base. USAF

Famous aviator Eddie Rickenbacker is briefed by Gen. Harry Johnson, commander of the Shemya Air Force Base in 1944. USAF

The village of Atka, which was rebuilt after the war. Aleuts from Attu were moved here. Most of the Atka elders died after they were evacuated to southeastern Alaska. Atka was the Russian headquarters for the western Aleutians when they owned Alaska. *USA*

Atka harbor, with the cemetery at the left. The Navy stationed PBYs here in the summer of 1942 for bombing runs to Kiska. The Japanese retaliated, but its June 12 bombing raid caused only negligible damage. The Aleut natives were ordered to evacuate the village and the Navy burned it to the ground to prevent its use by the enemy. *USA*

Vice Rear Adm. Thomas C. Kinkaid, commander of naval forces in the Aleutian area, talks with troops on Adak Island in August 1943. He took over from Rear Adm. Robert E. Theobald in January 1943 and conducted the successful naval war against the Japanese.　　　USA

Some of the American and Canadian staff officers who helped direct the Aleutian Campaign in 1943. Left to right: Brig. Gen. F. L. Whittaker, Maj. K. W. MacIntyre, Col. H. Allen, Gen. S. B. Buckner, Maj. Gen. G. R. Pearkes, Capt. B. E. Cowant, Lt. W. Shield and Col. E. C. Gault.　　　USA

Surplus metal drums on Shemya Island. Drums of this type, which were scattered from Attu in the Aleutians clear across Alaska and northern Canada to Norman Wells, provided a gigantic disposal problem after the war.

USAF

Jane Geitner of the American Red Cross writes a letter home for a wounded airman at Shemya in 1944.

Jane Geitner Tucker
Old Tappan, N.J.

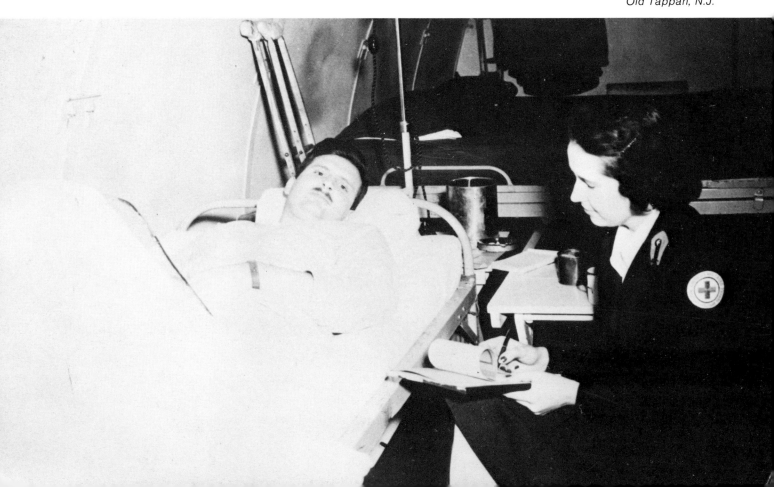

Two man light tanks of the Provisional Tank Company of the 138th Infantry Regiment maneuver in a mountain pass near Fort Glenn, Umnak Island, 1942. Most areas of the Aleutians were not suited to tank operations. *USA*

An anti-tank battery practices in an Aleutian mountain pass. *NA*

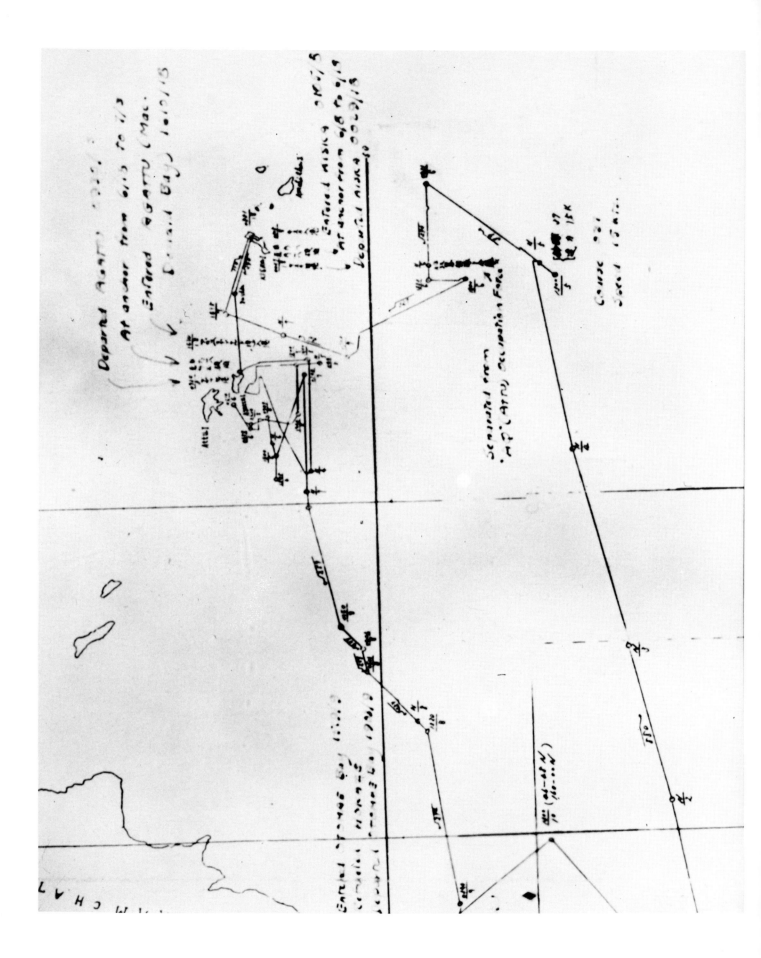

Map 10
Captured Japanese map of the Aleutian Islands' invasion force.

AHL

122

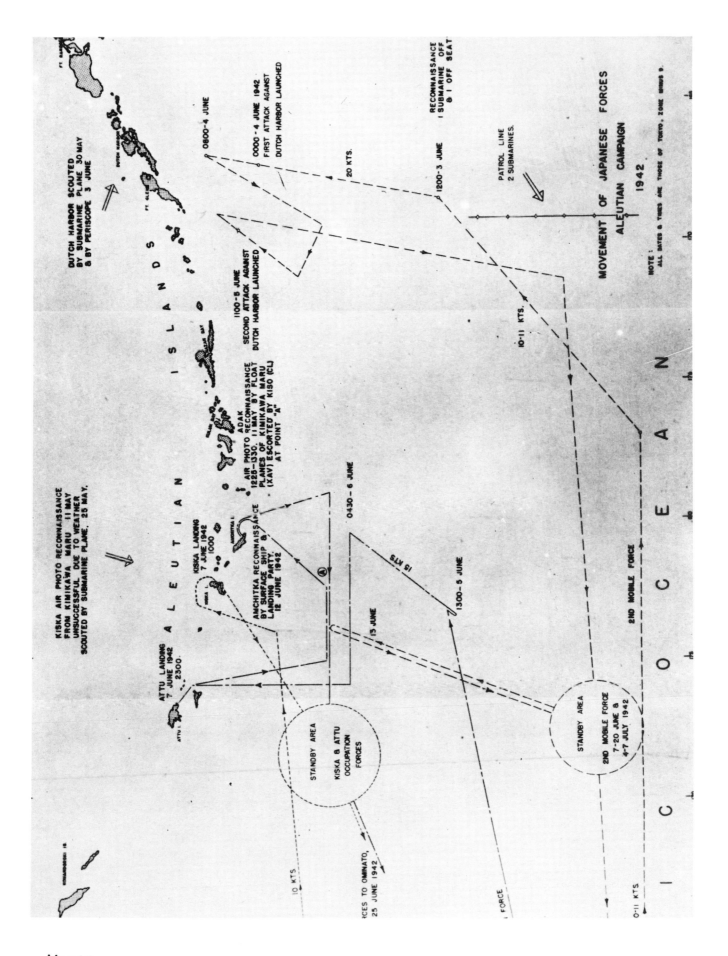

Map 11
Movement of Japanese forces in the Aleutian Campaign, 1942.

AHL

123

Fort Mears afire after the Japanese attack on Dutch Harbor, June 3, 1942.　　　　USN

DUTCH HARBOR
NO SECOND PEARL HARBOR

Dutch Harbor is on the small island of Amaknak, just across Illiuliuk Bay from the historic village of Unalaska. It is 850 air miles from Anchorage and almost due north of Honolulu. Unalaska was an important crossroads during the Russian occupation (1741-1867) and Dutch Harbor was an important coaling station and supply point for naval vessels of the Bering Sea fleet and for whalers and sealers. During the Klondike and Nome gold rushes (1897-1900) the area was important as a stopover for shipping to and from Seattle and St. Michaels near the mouth of the Yukon River. After 1900 Dutch Harbor became almost a ghost town; its only claim to fame was that it had the only brick building in the Aleutians. Tradition says a Dutch ship was the first to use its harbor. The Russians called the place Udokta. The Americans first called it Lincoln Harbor in the 1890s.

Before the Pearl Harbor attack, Gen. Buckner had obtained money for an army base, Fort Mears, near Dutch Harbor. A naval base there was commissioned in September 1941.[1] The submarine base was in operation by April 1942, but facilities for both surface and undersea craft were incomplete at the time of the Japanese attack on June 3, 1942.

After the Pearl Harbor attack, the U.S. Navy still had its aircraft carriers. Japanese Adm. Yamamoto was wary of them, and to make sure they were not steaming toward Japan, he set out radio-equipped fishing boats on a picket line, 600 to 700 miles east of the Japanese coast. He also used aircraft to extend his patrol line.

To draw the American carriers out into battle, Yamamoto proposed a joint sweep against Midway Island, only 1,300 miles from Hawaii, and the Aleutians. His patrol line would then extend from the Aleutians south to Midway, give him greater security, and possibly draw the carriers into battle where the superior Japanese forces would annihilate them.

The main thrust was to be at Midway. A diversionary attack on Dutch Harbor was designed to draw off the American carriers. The Japanese hoped that the ensuing occupation of several islands of the Aleutians would break the Russian-American supply line, furnish patrol bases to guard Japan's northern flank, and provide a possible invasion route into Canada and the western United States.

Japan's Naval General Staff, however, wanted to invade Australia first, for Japanese forces were almost at Australia's shores in the spring of 1942.[2]

Yamamoto had a hard time persuading the General Staff to follow his plan. A single raid helped Yamamoto change the others' thinking, and altered the course of the war.

On April 18, 1942, bombs rained down on Tokyo from 16 B-25 Mitchell bombers led by Lt. Col. James Doolittle. Although damage was slight, the raid showed that Japan was vulnerable to attack, and clamor arose for destruction of the enemy and protection of the homeland. Some Japanese thought the bombers had come from the Aleutians. In fact, they had flown off the **U.S.S. Hornet** 700 miles off the Japanese mainland.

On May 5, 1942, the Japanese General Headquarters issued Navy Order #18. It directed the commander-in-chief of the Combined Fleet to:

"Invade and occupy Midway Island and key points in the western Aleutians in cooperation with the Army, in order to prevent enemy task forces from making attacks against the homeland.

"Destroy all enemy forces that may oppose the invasion."

Japan's plan, called AO, was to destroy Dutch Harbor and occupy Attu, Kiska and Adak islands. The Second Carrier Striking Force under command of Adm. Kakuta headed toward the Aleutians in late May, while Yamamoto's southern fleet steamed toward Midway. The northern force would strike first on June 3, the southern the next day.

The Aleutian striking force was composed of the carriers **Ryujo** and **Junyo**, heavy cruisers **Maya** and **Takas** and three destroyers. In addition there were transports holding 2,500 troops for the island occupations. Five I-class submarines were also included to scout the waters from Kodiak to Attu.

Japan's plan for a feint toward the Aleutians did not fool the Americans, as they had earlier broken the top-secret Japanese Naval code ("Purple Code") and had a good idea of what the enemy was up to.

At Dutch Harbor an attack was expected. After Pearl Harbor all naval and air bases within striking range of Japanese forces were on constant alert.[3] The enemy would attack the base with

[2]In fact Japanese bombers had raided Darwin in northern Australia on Feb. 12, 1942 causing some damage.

[1]A U.S. Navy wireless station was established at Dutch Harbor in 1912. Congress appropriated $40 million for Navy and Army bases there in 1941.

[3]A PBY from VP-42 sighted the Japanese carriers during the first day's attack and radioed for help, but apparently his message did not get through as no bombers came.

Pre-war views of Dutch Harbor and Unalaska.

UW

little up-to-date intelligence on the facilities there and with no knowledge of the two secret bases at Umnak and Cold Bay that had fighters to protect the naval facilities.[4]

Early on the morning of June 3, the enemy fleet steamed within 170 miles of Dutch Harbor. Fighters and bombers took off from both carriers

for the initial attack. Sixteen planes from **Ryujo** reached their target, but weather prevented **Junyo's** planes from completing their mission. The Americans also had problems. A radio message to Fort Glenn on Umnak Island, warning of the attack did not get through, so no U.S. fighters took off on the first day of the attack.[5]

American destroyers were spotted in Makushin Bay on the west coast of Unalaska Island, and 24

---

[1]The Japanese were using maps that were 30 years old and had no recent aerial photographs of the base. They assumed that there were no land-based fighters and that they would have to deal only with a few PBYs. The new airfields of Umnak and Cold Bay had not been discovered by June 3.

[5]Jack Chennault's squadron of P-40s and a few bombers were waiting on Umnak for the expected attack. It learned about the first day's battle after it was over.

Aerial view of Dutch Harbor in 1942 before the Japanese attack.　　　RC

enemy planes took off to try to sink them. Again the weather interfered. The planes could not find the destroyers.

Dutch Harbor had been hit (for twenty minutes), but other than doing some damage to Fort Mears, where 25 soldiers died, and damaging the radio station and oil tanks, the raid was unsuccessful. One PBY had been shot up while trying to take off, and another was shot down 200 miles south of Dutch Harbor on June 3. Three of the crew were picked up by the Japanese. Four enemy float planes from the cruisers were off course and found themselves over Umnak Island. Two were shot down and the remaining two made it back to their ships with no idea where the American land based fighters had come from.

Kakuta wanted to attack Adak on June 4, but weather closed in so he decided to launch a second attack on Dutch Harbor.

The attack on June 4 was stronger than the first and inflicted much more damage on shore installations and an old beached ship, the **S. S. Northwestern**. There were dogfights between the attacking aircraft and planes from Umnak. The Americans spotted the Japanese fleet and PBYs and B-26 bombers tried many times to sink the enemy carriers, but to no avail.

By now the battle of Midway was on and in a few hours would become a major Japanese defeat. Yamamoto radioed to his northern fleet to steam south immediately, but the order was received too late. The planes had left their carriers for the second attack on Dutch Harbor.

With the battle of Midway lost, Yamamoto wanted to abandon the Aleutian venture, but was talked into continuing the effort to salvage some measure of victory. Kakuta decided not to occupy Dutch Harbor or Adak, as they were too far from his supply lines and too close to possible American bases. Instead he proceeded to the western Aleutians to occupy Attu and Kiska.

American losses in the Dutch Harbor battle were 78 men killed and 14 planes downed. The Japanese lost 15 men and less than a dozen planes.

The loss of one of the Japanese Zeros proved to be disastrous to future Zero pilots. The plane's oil line was severed by a bullet from a

Fort Mears under construction at Dutch Harbor in August 1941.　　　　　　NA

PBY. Losing oil pressure, the pilot radioed that he would put down at a pre-arranged site on Akutan Island to be picked up by a submarine. The pilot came in for a crash landing with his wheels down, not knowing that he was landing in soft muskeg. The wheels caught and flipped the plane over, killing the pilot.

Thirty days later, the crashed Zero, still in good condition, was spotted and after three salvage attempts was brought back to Dutch Harbor and transported back to the States. It was rebuilt and test flown to give engineers a better idea of how to design a plane to counter the Zero's great maneuverability.

On Kiska the morning of June 7, Japanese forces stormed ashore and fired on the little American weather station. The 10 sailors manning the station ran into the hills for cover, but all but one were captured within a few days. Ens. William House, the commander of the detachment, managed to hide out for 49 days before he had to surrender because of hunger. All the prisoners were taken to Japan and spent the rest of the war there. They all returned home after the war.

At Attu on the same day, the Japanese transports steamed into Massacre Bay and discharged 1,200 troops. The troops rushed into Chichagof Village and captured all 39 Aleut villagers. Mr. and Mrs. Charles Foster Jones, Bureau of Indian Affairs representatives on the island and the only whites there, were as surprised as the natives. Charles Jones tapped out a radio signal that they were being overrun and then tried to make a run for it. He was gunned down by the enemy soldiers, the only person killed in the invasion. His wife was taken prisoner and with the rest of the natives was eventually sent to Japan for the duration of the war.

With the loss of communications from both islands it was assumed that they had been overrun. On June 10 a bomber from the 36th Bombardment Squadron discovered the Japanese entrenched on the islands.

The Navy in the meantime had been searching everywhere for the elusive enemy fleet, but by the time the Japanese were discovered on Attu and Kiska, the fleet was hundreds of miles away heading back home. The weather again, as it would do so many times in the future, had obscured the movements of the opposing forces.

"When I arrived at Dutch Harbor in the early fall of 1941, it little resembled an air station. As a matter of fact, it reminded me more of a large construction camp. Civilians and Army personnel were quite prominent but Navy was some-what conspicuous by its absence. As time passed tho, Navy gradually came into its own. Squadrons of patrol bombers with large ground crews and ever increasing numbers of submarines and surface vessels made an appearance.

"As Corey Ford, Senator Chandler, Life Magazine and others wrote rather loosely of the Navy's major Aleutian base pre-June third and post-June third days, it struck me that there must be other angles to the story.

"Mr. Ford elaborated on the enormous salaries the civilian workers were receiving which was quite true. He also called attention to how the civilians could afford and did partake of some unknown quantities of liquor in the prominent Unalaska Bars but when he remarked that the soldiers and sailors hovered in the background awaiting their turn at the bar and then to merely purchase beer, I had 'visible' reason to doubt that statement. True, on their meager incomes, soldiers and sailors could not possibly afford to play too many return engagements during any one month with the exception of a very few, but beer was not all they drank on these occasions.

"Senator Chandler, a member of a senatorial investigation party, visiting the Aleutians after June third and fourth, 1942, remained there all of three hours. Naturally the day or maybe I should say time of the day they arrived and departed, it remained quite clear of fog; disproving the Aleutian 'Bug-a-boo'. If just a few of the many dead that have been in planes that have flown into mountains could talk, I'm sure they as well as the living Alaskan airmen would be willing to argue this point.

"It was also ascertained that Dutch Harbor would have fallen had the Japanese pressed their advantage, 'Air Superiority' but I for one doubt it.

"There was also the cry of another 'Pearl Harbor.' 'No Alarm Sounded.' It is obviously silly to sound the general alarm, calling men to their stations when all hands were already at these battle stations and had been from the wee hours in the a.m. As a matter of fact, the manning of battle stations from the wee hours in the a.m. until secure was sounded was routine and had been for some time."

Clinton H. Dutcher
Inverness, Florida

"I was a doctor at Dutch Harbor in 1943, temporarily attached to the 250th Coast Artillery. Our biggest problem after the Japanese were expelled from the Aleutians was having something to do. Most of the hospital cases were the normal ailments, accidents, skin diseases from the cold and damp and some self-inflicted wounds.

An artilleryman came in one day to get a routine circumcision, partially out of boredom and partially because of health reasons. This operation, although minor in nature, does immobilize the patient for a number of days.

Word got out to other platoons and soon I was performing three to four operations a day. I was happy to get the surgical practice and it relieved boredom on my part too.

During this period when so many men were in the hospital, the commanding officer of the artillery unit called for a trial alert to test his defenses. Some of the guns could not be manned properly because so many men were immobilized.

Needless to say, the commanding officer was very upset and orders were issued that only one man from a platoon could be circumcised at a time."

Dr. C.P. Brooke
Missoula, Montana

Headlines tell of the Japanese assault.

University of Montana Library

Japanese bombs fall harmlessly in the harbor.

NA

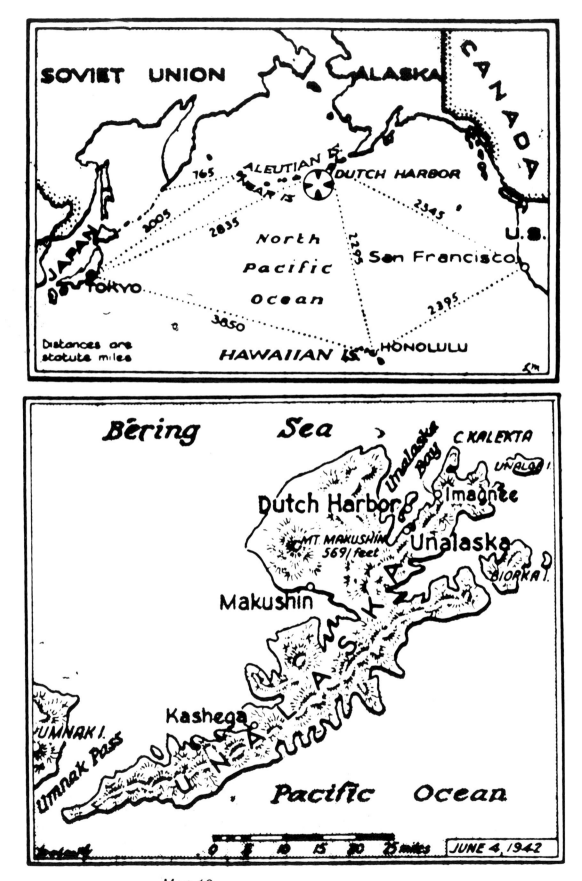

Map 12
Unalaska Island and Dutch Harbor.

132

Troops in trenches during the first attack on Dutch Harbor, June 3, 1942. Most were still wearing World War I helmets.   NA

A tank farm at Dutch Harbor burns after the first attack. The water reservoir is in the foreground, the radio station in the background.   USN

The Japanese carrier **Ryujo,** *flagship of the strike force in the North Pacific. Her 16 fighter and torpedo bombers bombed Dutch Harbor on June 3 and 4, 1942.* Official Japanese Navy Photo

The **S.S. Northwestern,** *an old Alaskan Steamship Company freighter had earlier been beached in the harbor and was being used as a barracks for civilian construction workers. It was hit on June 4 and partially burned.* UAA

A bomb went through the roof of the seaplane hangar.   RC

The hospital at Unalaska was badly damaged on June 4.   RC

Dutch Harbor on June 27, 1942. Because of a lack of up-to-date intelligence information, the Japanese caused only slight damage to the military installations. NA

A U.S. submarine is welcomed with cheers and band music at Dutch Harbor on its return from a Pacific patrol. NA

A snowstorm at Dutch Harbor on Aug. 8, 1942. A PBY and a lone sentry are on the runway. NA

Soldiers entertain soldiers at Dutch Harbor in January 1945. NA

Adak Airbase in 1943.

Frank Harvey
Haddon Heights, N.J.

ADAK
THE BASTION OF
THE ISLANDS

Adak is an extremely rugged island 435 miles west of Dutch Harbor and 275 miles east of Kiska. Numerous mountains reach 2,000 feet above sea level, with Mount Moffett at 3,924 feet dominating the island. The shoreline is generally rocky and rugged, giving scant shelter from storms in the Bering Sea and Pacific Ocean. Annual rainfall is about 75 inches, October and November are the wettest months. Snow, while not extreme, can fall anytime between December and May. Temperatures can vary from 18°F to 72°F and wind velocities reach well over 100 miles per hour. Fog and ice are common here as on other islands.

After the Japanese occupied Kiska in June 1942, American bombers had to attack them from airfields at Umnak or Cold Bay, hundreds of miles away. It was important that an airfield closer to Kiska be found. By a quirk of fate, the Japanese, after the attack on Dutch Harbor, had decided to occupy Kiska and Attu rather than Adak. The Americans jumped at the chance to

Members of the Army Nurse Corps stand in front of their Quonset quarters in 1943.   USA

obtain this island for a base as it was only 275 miles east of Kiska.[1]

The island was thought to be unoccupied by the enemy, but the Japanese were known to send out frequent patrols. On the nights of Aug. 27 and 28, 1942, Castner's Alaska Scouts landed from rubber boats to reconnoiter the island. Finding the island unoccupied, they flashed a message to the invasion force to land.

A strange flotilla approached the island. It was made up of scows, yachts, schooners, barges, tugs, purse-seiners and a few naval vessels. The Navy at this time was short of vessels and anything that could float was used. The landing force of troops and aviation engineers started construction of what was to become the major military base in the Aleutians.

Their main objective was to build an airfield

On the morning after the greatest recorded storm in Aleutian history in April 1943, an officer stands outside his Quonset hut on Adak. The island's wind-measuring anemometer broke when a 110 mile-per-hour gust struck it. How much harder the wind blew after that was anyone's guess.   USAF

[1]The Army had initially wanted to build an airbase on Tanaga Island to the west but the Navy opted for Adak because of the better harbor facilities. Only five islands in the Aleutians can accommodate large naval vessels: Akun, Unalaska, Adak, Kiska and Massacre Bay at Attu.

as fast as possible in order to provide security against enemy fighters and seaplanes operating from Kiska and to keep up the bombing missions over Kiska. All initial construction efforts were concentrated on this airfield. Col. Benjamin Talley, the senior engineer of the Alaska Defense Force, was in charge of the initial construction.

There was one possible airfield site at Sweeper Cove Lagoon in the lower valley of the island.[2] At low tide this site provided a smooth surface but it filled with water at high tide. A creek also inundated the area. Dikes were built to control the creek and a tidal gate or dam was built at the entrance of the lagoon to control the tidal water. When dry, the site was a fine airfield with a hard sand surface. After the drying out phase, 2,700 feet of perforated steel landing mat, 100 feet wide, was laid down. Just 14 days after the first landings, bombers were able to take off for runs over Kiska, and fighters could be brought in to protect the area.

On Oct. 1 an enemy Zero reconnoitered the island, and several days later a lone plane dropped a few bombs, without causing much damage. This was the last enemy action against Adak.

After the original runway was completed, engineer units went to work on additional runways, taxiways and hardstands. Heavy construction equipment was needed to complete these projects. Much sand had to be found and dispersed over the runways to make a base for the steel runway mats.

As this was the major base in the Aleutians, housing and other facilities had to be built to house up to 90,000 men who passed through on their way to the invasions of Attu and Kiska and to other construction projects in the area.

While the Army was establishing its base in the late summer of 1942, Navy Seabees landed and built a naval airfield, dock facilities, torpedo nets and areas for PBY use.[3] They also established a radio control station that provided instant communications with naval headquarters at Kodiak and with ships and aircraft throughout the island chain.

By May 1943, the island was fully garrisoned and was a virtual island battleship and supply depot. It was ready for the invasion of Japanese held islands to the west.

---

[2]One of the Alaska Scouts who had trapped on the island had remembered this site as being flat and pointed it out as a possible airfield site.

[3]The naval airfield built on Adak was named Albert Mitchell Field after Ens. A. E. Mitchell who was shot down by Japanese fighters during the Dutch Harbor attack. In September 1945, it was placed in caretaker status, and all Navy operations were conducted from the Army field.

Sweeper Cove on Adak, showing the site of the new airfield in 1942. This view is looking north.

141   RC

The 807th Engineer Aviation Battalion unloads in Sweeper Cove in August 1942. Adak was occupied by American forces on Aug. 28. USA

Soldiers line up for Sunday church services at Adak in February 1943. USA

The housing area at Adak was usually a sea of mud and water, especially in 1942 and early 1943.

USAF

P-40E (left) and AT-6 (right) parked at Adak.

Frank Harvey
Haddon Heights, N.J.

Adak in August 1943. The airfield is in the right background and ships in the harbor are ready for the upcoming invasion of Kiska.   RC

Housing on Adak in 1944. By the spring of 1943 Adak was the largest base in the Aleutians and the staging area for the reconquest of Attu and Kiska islands.   FR

Safety posters used in the Aleutian campaign.

D. W. McKay
Little Rock, Arkansas

Soldiers fight the wind as they pitch a tent.

AMCHITKA
CLOSE ENOUGH TO SEE
THEIR CAMPFIRES

Lying only 60 miles east of Kiska, Amchitka appeared to be an ideal site for an air base. It was close enough to both of the occupied islands of Attu and Kiska to be a base for round-the-clock bombing and a springboard for invasion. It was thought to be unoccupied, and this was confirmed by a scouting expedition in December 1942. Signs that an enemy survey party had been there were found.

The island is long, hilly and shaped somewhat like a gravy boat. Its pre-war population was a large herd of sea otters.

The Joint Chiefs of Staff had ordered the island occupied, and Adm. Kinkaid had assembled a small flotilla of three cruisers, four destroyers and four transports to deliver 2,100 engineers and other troops.

Jan. 5, 1943, was supposed to be the landing day, but because of bad weather the landing was postponed until the morning of Jan. 12. The storm slackened just enough for landings to begin.

A detachment of Alaska Scouts was to go ashore in Constantine Harbor from the destroyer **U.S.S. Worden.** The ship got into the harbor and discharged the Scouts, but trying to leave she was dashed against a pinnacle rock, split open and sank. Fourteen sailors drowned.

Weather conditions were terrible that day, but the transports managed to unload their troops without further incident.

Amchitka was no picnic for the occupation force. Men spent their energy fighting the cold, snow, wind and frozen muskeg. Winds of 100 miles an hour, blowing from every direction, even made it hard to urinate.

Because of the bad weather a few days passed before the Japanese discovered the American presence. When they did they tried to blast them off the island. On an average of every three days for several weeks they bombed the airfield under construction, but inflicted only a few casualties. Once adequate antiaircraft guns were in place and fighters could land on the island, enemy action ceased. After Feb. 18, the only sign of what was thought to be the enemy was a flight of geese that had everybody scampering for cover. A Navy pilot said it was the first time he had seen enemy planes flapping their wings.

Under protection of fighter planes, the engineers soon created a runway that could be used by medium bombers, and by March the runway was long enough for heavy bombers.[1]

Like other bases, Amchitka was built on a round-the-clock schedule in weather that would have precluded work in pre-war times. Sand and gravel for the runway had to be hauled in from borrow pits two miles away. This was done even at night under floodlights, with the enemy only 60 miles away.

Living conditions for the plane crews and troops were poor. Mud was much more of a problem than enemy planes. Water seeping through the muskeg was everywhere. Food supplies were limited at first, but did improve as more facilities were built. Constantine Harbor facilities were improved. With a base this close to the enemy, the battle for Attu and Kiska could begin in earnest.

---

[1] Jack Chennault's P-40 squadron flew into the island on Jan. 28. Ten P-38 fighter-bombers came in next and in March the 36th Bombardment squadron moved its headquarters to the island.

An American gunner cleans his machine gun beside the Amchitka graveyard.   USA

Food dumps along Infantry Road looking north on Amchitka Island, March 2, 1943.　　USA

The interior of a tent on Amchitka. Living conditions were no better than other bases on the chain--tents, cold, wet weather and mud.　　USA

A sand dump used for runway and dispersal area construction on Amchitka Island. The runway was ready for use two weeks after the island was occupied. *USAF*

Paratroopers of the 1st Special Service Force stand by a transport plane at Amchitka. They were ready for a jump into Kiska, but were not needed after the enemy evacuated the island.
Robert Durkee
Helena, Montana

P-40s of Jack Chennault's command are ready at the taxiway for a possible encounter with Japanese bombers in March 1943.   USA

An indicator as to how strong the wind blows in the Aleutians is shown in this picture made at the 11th Air Force Base on Amchitka. Wind whipping in off the Bering Sea lifted this heavy steel runway matting (Marston mat) off a frozen snow covered hardstand at the edge of a runway and twisted it into a giant coil. Approximately 3,500 square feet of matting weighing eight tons was rolled by the wind.   USAF

The U.S.S. Tennesssee at anchor in Adak harbor just before the Kiska invasion.   USA

THE NAVY
AT WAR
FIGHTING ENEMY AND
WEATHER

The U.S. Navy has been in Alaska most of the time since 1887. Through the years naval commanders insisted they could defend Alaska without the Army's help. General disinterest by the American government in the early 20th century precluded any large-scale military development in Alaska.

The Washington Naval Conference Treaty of 1922 stopped all naval construction in the Aleutians. The Depression of the 1930s further militated against appropriations.

The Navy was not completely inactive, however. In 1904, Kiska was set aside as a naval reserve. A small base was started there in 1916, but was soon abandoned. A wireless station had been established at Dutch Harbor in 1912. In the early 1930s several surveys were made of the Aleutians.

Adm. Arthur Hepburn headed a board charged with expanding naval aviation in the 1930s. It recommended that 15 facilities be built in the United States and its territories, including naval air stations at Sitka and Kodiak. On April 25, 1939, $2.9 million was authorized for Sitka and $8.7 million for Kodiak.

Dutch Harbor was not even authorized as a naval base until 1941, and was not completed at the time of the Japanese attack on June 3, 1942.

Kodiak was to become the main naval base in Alaska because of its strategic location and because it could harbor the fleet. It was not completed at the time of Pearl Harbor. A hangar and runway were completed and docks and revetments were being built along with artillery emplacements.

In 1941 an article about the Aleutian Islands in the U.S. Naval Institute Proceedings stated: "At this time no charts exist of the great majority of the Aleutian indentations and many of those that do exist cannot be trusted."

A further article in the Proceedings talked about the dangers of navigation: "Many of these dangerous pinnacles have been found through disastrous shipwrecks. The straits between the islands vary in width from yards to several miles. They are deep, but are dotted with occasional pinnacles and other unmarked dangers. Currents in the straits are often swift and erratic. While there are differences in the islands, it is extremely difficult to tell them apart even after long experience. When to this is added the ever-present fog, concealing the coast and foothills of one island and the tops and peaks of the next, it is apparent that navigation about the islands is not an unmixed pleasure."

After Pearl Harbor all of Alaska was in a state of war emergency. All military dependents were ordered to leave, and 250 women and children were taken from Dutch Harbor. Even the prostitutes left. More than 700 persons were evacuated from Kodiak. Ships sailed up and down the Inside Passage and across the Gulf of Alaska without destroyer escort. Japanese submarines were reported in Alaskan waters, but they did not attack the civilian ships.

At Anchorage, an officer looked over a map and said: "Here we are perched in a hard country where civilians can't feed themselves. The Japs don't even have to attack. They need only use subs to cut our umbilical cord from Seattle, and we'll be starved to death."

In October 1940, Capt. Ralph C. Parker was placed in charge of the newly created Alaskan Sector of the Seattle Naval District. His flagship was the **U.S.S. Charleston,** the only vessel in the Alaska Navy. Parker leased a few private fishing boats and pleasure craft to patrol the Alaska

Rear Adm. Robert A. Theobald, commander of the North Pacific Fleet in Alaskan waters until he was relieved on Jan. 4, 1943, by Adm. Thomas Kinkaid. USN

154

Coast. This part of his navy was called the Yard Patrol or "Yippie Boats."

After Pearl Harbor, his fleet was reinforced with a few old destroyers, some ships of the Royal Canadian Navy and three Coast Guard cutters. Several submarines arrived at Dutch Harbor late in January for patrol work.

Adm. Chester Nimitz, commander in chief of the Pacific Fleet, (CINCPAC) decided to add additional naval units to protect Alaska and created the North Pacific Force with Rear Adm. Robert A. Theobald in command. Theobald arrived at Kodiak on May 27, 1942, aboard his flagship the **U.S.S. Nashville.** There was an immediate clash of personalities with Buckner, whom he met there. The tension continued throughout the campaign and hindered operations to some degree.

With the Japanese fast approaching Dutch Harbor in June, Theobald's five cruisers and four destroyers were deployed around Kodiak and Dutch Harbor. However, the battle turned out to be strictly an aerial fight between American and Japanese planes.

One of the most important naval units that did not arrive in Alaska until after the attack on Dutch Harbor was the Seabees--the construction arm of the Navy. The first battalion to be trained was on a train going through Texas, headed for the South Pacific, when it was diverted to Alaska.

It was the forerunners of many battalions that would build some of the enormous facilities in the Aleutians.

PBYs

The PBYs (Catalinas) first deployed in Alaska became the workhorse of the Navy there. They were designed to be patrol planes but ended up being used extensively as bombers.

VP-41 squadron of Navy Patrol Wing 4 was deployed to Alaska in 1941. It was returned to Oregon for a short period in early 1942. VP-42 was also deployed to Alaska in 1942. The planes were rotated among three bases, Kodiak, Sitka and Dutch Harbor. The 12 planes had to cover 2,400 miles of Alaska coast.

During the Dutch Harbor attack, the squadron was in the thick of the combat. One PBY had found the Japanese carriers but was shot down and three of the crew were taken prisoners, the first of the Aleutian campaign. Another PBY found the carriers on June 3 but his radio message was garbled and did not get through. Several other planes were lost to enemy action.

After the Japanese occupied Kiska on June 7, the 11th Air Force tried to drive the enemy off.

Its failure prompted Navy Patrol Wing 4 Commander Leslie Gehres to propose that his 20 PBY's stationed at Atka try their luck.

PBYs were not built for this kind of action, however. They were slow, hard to maneuver, and lightly armored and armed. Gehres' message to his men was clear, however: Bomb the enemy out of Kiska, or bomb regardless of weather until they ran out of fuel and bombs.

For three days the PYBs were in the air constantly, but took a savage beating. They in turn were inflicting losses on the enemy, sinking three "Mavis" flying boats in the harbor and scoring hits on several ships. With half the planes lost, fuel and ammunition almost exhausted and intercepted Japanese communications indicating a possible attack on Atka, Adm. Nimitz ordered the "Kiska Blitz" to halt.

On June 14, enemy planes flew over Atka and bombed the village, but all the inhabitants and

A destroyer closes in on a transport to shoot a line aboard to take a message. A complete radio silence was observed, most of the signal work was accomplished through the use of blinkers. USA

155

navy personnel had already been evacuated.

A seaplane tender, the **U.S.S. Casco,** was torpedoed by a Japanese submarine in Nazan Bay, Atka, on Aug. 29, 1942. PBYs from VP-42 and 43 along with the destroyer **U.S.S. Reid** sank the sub and took five prisoners. The **Casco** was beached with her forward engine room blown out, but was eventually refloated and repaired.

After the occupation of Adak in August 1942, VP-42 had its base of operations there.

VP-43 squadron, which earlier had been stationed in Alaska, returned to duty in Alaska in October 1943 and was stationed on Attu and Shemya islands. It made the first night raid on the Japanese Kurile Islands, and during the next 23 months made many photoreconnaissance flights and bombing missions.

During the war in Alaska, PBYs and PV-1 Ventura bombers flew 704 combat sorties and thousands of patrols. They dropped 295 tons of bombs. Sixteen planes were lost in combat, 35 in accidents.

BATTLE OF THE KOMANDORSKIS

Adm. Theobald was replaced by Adm. Thomas Kinkaid in January 1943. Kinkaid immediately went on the offensive. With every ship he could gather, he formed a blockade squadron to try to stop Japanese ships from reaching the garrisons on Kiska and Attu. The ships patrolled far out to the sea opposite the Kurile Islands and managed to sink or turn back the Japanese transports. Adm. "Soc" McMorris had command of this small but effective force.

A transport that reached Attu on March 10, was the last to run the blockade. The defenses on Attu were in serious trouble, and without heavy construction equipment they could not complete the airfield from which land-based fighters and bombers could operate.

The Japanese high command decided to send a large naval task force with transports to break the blockade and reinforce the islands. On March 26, 1943, the Americans intercepted the enemy off the Russian Komandorskis Islands. It produced the longest continuous gunnery duel in modern naval history and was the last significant naval action in the Aleutian campaign.

Although the heavy cruiser **U.S.S.Salt Lake City** was nearly sunk and the American fleet was out-gunned, the Japanese broke off the engagement and headed home in the belief that they were being attacked by heavy bombers. Thus the blockade held and it was just a matter of time before the Japanese garrisons would be starved out.

BATTLE OF THE PIPS

A strange battle in July 1943 led to the suc-

The flagship cruiser **U.S.S.Salt Lake City** *before it went dead in the water at the Battle of the Komandorskis in the North Pacific on March 26, 1943. The 3½ hour battle was the longest continuous duel between surface ships in modern naval history. The battle was a major American victory. The* **Salt Lake City** *eventually got up steam and returned to Dutch Harbor.*

USN

156

cessful evacuation of the Japanese garrison on Kiska. Seven pips were detected on radar screens southwest of Attu by U.S. Navy ships. These were thought to be enemy transports, bringing in reinforcements for Kiska. Two destroyers that had been blockading Kiska Harbor were ordered to race for the radar contact along with the North Pacific Fleet but no contact was made. The fleet turned back toward Kiska and again spotted seven pips on radar screens. On July 26 the Americans opened fire on what they thought might be Japanese transports.

In fact the evacuation fleet at that moment was hundreds of miles to the south, waiting for fog to cover its dash for Kiska Harbor. With the American fleet moving away from Kiska to refuel and rearm, the way was open for the successful evacuation.

No one has ever determined what the ships were firing at. The radar screens of the battleships had all shown seven pips and they all converged on one point. It could have been enemy submarines running on the surface as a feint, or merely a phenomenon of unusual atmospheric conditions. Whatever it was, it worked to the enemy's advantage.

After the Kiska invasion the North Pacific Fleet was reduced in size and deployed in the Kurile Islands area to bottle up the Japanese fleet and bombard island bases. Although the force had mainly obsolete ships, it controlled the seas for the next two years losing 15 ships while sinking 30 of the enemy's ships.

Officers aboard the **U.S.S. Pennsylvania** *at Adak on Aug. 7, 1943. Lt. Col. James Roosevelt, son of the President, was in this group. The* **Pennsylvania** *took part in the Attu invasion.*

AHFAM

A PT boat in Kodiak Harbor in April 1943. They were sent to the Aleutians in hopes that their speed and maneuverability could inflict serious damage on enemy ships. They proved useless in the rough seas and bad weather.

NA

A destroyer aground in Adak harbor in 1944. A storm with winds in excess of 140 mph was responsible. An earth ramp was built to unload stores, ammunition and fuel. It took several weeks to refloat her.

Frank Harvey
Haddon Heights, N.J.

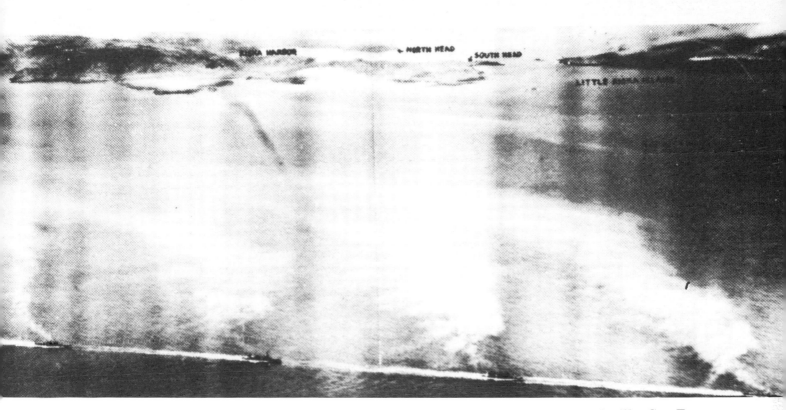

Four cruisers bombard Kiska on July 23, 1943. Left to right: **U.S.S.Santa Fe, Louisville, San Francisco** and **Wichita.**

USN

U.S. Army tracked vehicles move forward over a dirt ramp on Attu after emerging from an LST (landing ship-tank). The huge doors that opened in the bow of the ship permitted rapid landing of men and equipment. These ships were used all over the world during the war.

NA

A Japanese transport, hit by a U.S. bomber, sinks in flames in the waters of the western Aleutian Chain.　　　　　　　　　　　　　　　　　　　　　　　　　　　　*NA*

A U.S. Coast Guard cutter on patrol. The Coast Guard performed numerous duties on the sea and in the air during the Aleutian Campaign.　　　　　　　　　　　　　　　　　　*NA*

B runway and taxiway on Attu in February 1944. Casco Cove is in the background. PBYs and PV-1s took off from here for their raids on the Kurile Islands.
Jack Haugen
San Leandro, California

A PBY flipped on its back after being caught in a williwaw (severe wind storm common in the Aleutians).
USN

Remains of a PBY that crashed into Mount Moffett on Adak in 1943.

Frank Harvey
Haddon Heights, N.J.

When fog closed in on Adak, this PBY landed in the dark in the open sea and taxied to the beach on Atka.

R.L. White
Lynn Haven, Florida

28-9

Storm conditions at Amchitka on Dec. 26, 1943.

Jack Haugen
San Leandro, California

A Navy PV-1 Ventura bomber over an Aleutian island.

Jack Haugen
San Leandro, California

Maj. Milton Askins, commanding officer of the 54th Fighter Squadron, briefs his new P-38 pilots before a run over Kiska in 1942.

USA

THE AIR FORCE AT WAR
WIND, FOG AND ICE

Four DeHavilland DH-4 airplanes commanded by Capt. St. Clair Streett made a 9,320 mile round trip from New York, to Nome, Alaska in the summer of 1920. It was the first military flight in Alaska, instigated by Gen. Billy Mitchell. Many other flights of a military nature were made through the years in Alaska but it was not until 1940 that a permanent military air field was built and planes stationed there.

In the spring of 1939 the first appropriations were passed for Alaska's defense when $4 million was made available for an Army cold-weather experimental station at Fairbanks. This later became Ladd Field.

Although Gen. George Marshall, Army Chief of Staff at the time, endorsed a project for an air base at Anchorage, a House Committee cut the necessary funds from the Army supply bill in the spring of 1940. The War Department, through the United States Land Office, had acquired suitable land in May 1939, however, and a crew of 25 locally hired men began construction of Ft. Richardson-Elmendorf Field on June 8, 1940. This was the extent of construction progress

A prime example of a "Flying Tiger", Capt. Morgan A. Giffin. USAF

completed when the initial Alaska Defense Force arrived in Anchorage 19 days later.

Elmendorf Field was born when the first Air Corps personnel arrived for permanent assignment. Maj. Everett S. Davis and two enlisted crew members flew their B-10B bomber into Anchorage's municipal airport, Merrill Field, on Aug. 9, 1940.

Since no barracks or other facilities were available, the men pitched tents on an old homestead and established their headquarters in the farmhouse.

War Department General Order No. 9, issued December 12, 1940, named the military reservation located near Anchorage as Fort Richardson and designated the flying field there as Elmendorf Field.

The air base was organized on Feb. 23, 1941, two days after the 18th Pursuit Squadron arrived and began to assemble 20 P-36 aircraft that had been shipped in crates. Soon afterward, Maj. William O. Eareckson, who would become a legendary pilot in the Aleutian campaign, arrived with the 73rd and 36th Bomber Squadrons, flying obsolete B-18 bombers.

When Pearl Harbor was attacked the defense of Alaska was in the hands of 12 remaining P-36 fighters and 6 B-18 bombers. This was soon to change, however. Except for one costly land battle and several naval engagements, the war that developed in the Aleutians was fought mainly in the air.

Many air bases were built down the Aleutian Chain. The first two, Otter Point on Umnak Island and Cold Bay on the Alaska Peninsula, were built as protection for Dutch Harbor. The Adak airfield, built in August 1942, put bombers close to Kiska and Attu. Amchitka was occupied in January 1943 to provide a base even closer to the occupied islands. After Attu and Kiska were retaken, air bases were completed there for the offensive action against the Japanese Kurile Islands.

Shemya Island just east of Attu was considered an important site for an air base in early 1943. Just after the battle for Attu, an advanced party of Alaska Scouts landed on the island and found it deserted. On May 30, 1943, 2,500 troops landed and began construction of a large air base. It was to become the major base for nearly two years of bombing of the Kurile Islands. It was supposed to have been used by the new B-29 Superfortresses, but only one landed there before the war was over.

Army pilots had trouble navigating in Alaska because the extreme mineralization caused their compasses to behave erratically. Winter flying in the cold interior was not as bad as along the Aleutian Chain where there was much more fog, ice and wind.[1]

Fog may occur at any time. Every island and peninsula in the area is mountainous; the tops of many are snow-covered the year around, as are the long mountain ranges further inland. This feature and the fact that glaciers abound throughout the region contribute to the rapid cooling of the air as it passes over the mountains, with the ultimate result that low stratus cloud and fog conditions exist for long periods at a time. At other times, the normal nocturnal cooling produces fog which usually forms after midnight and persists until the following noon, or later, unless dispelled by clearing winds or dissipated by surface heating.

THE 11TH AIR FORCE

The 11th Air Force was the major air unit in Alaska during the war. It had started the war with four B-17s, 31 B-26s, a few obsolete B-18s and several squadrons of P-40 fighters.

Gen. William O. Butler took over command in the early spring of 1942, but until he left for the European War Theater in late 1943 he did not get along with either Gen. Buckner or Adm. Kinkaid.

All through the Aleutian campaign leading up to the retaking of Attu and Kiska, the 11th was in constant battle against both the enemy and the weather conditions. It paved the way for recapture of both islands by massive bombing. Its fighters and bombers chased the few remaining enemy planes from the sky early in the campaign and quickly gained complete air superiority.[2]

In the fall of 1943, veteran Air Force units were sent back to the States. The 36th Squadron had been in Alaska for 28 months. During the war the 11th flew over 3,600 combat sorties with a loss of 40 aircraft in combat and 174 to weather conditions and other causes. Another 192 aircraft were badly damaged. The 11th Air Force dropped more than seven million pounds of bombs.

Total losses for the Allies in the Aleutian campaign, including Navy planes, were 471 aircraft. The Japanese lost 269.

[1]At Dutch Harbor the humidity ranges from 70 to 100% and rain or snow falls 180 days out of the year.

[2]The last Japanese air raid on the Aleutians was on Oct. 13, 1943, when nine "Betty" bombers made a run on Attu but caused no damage. On Oct. 20, a PBY and a "Betty" fought the last aerial skirmish of the campaign in the islands.

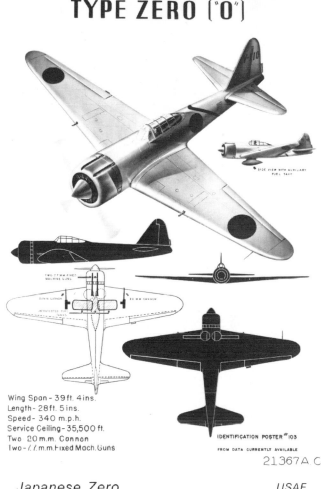

JAPANESE FIGHTER
TYPE ZERO ["O"]

Wing Span - 39 ft. 4 ins.
Length - 28 ft. 5 ins.
Speed - 340 m.p.h.
Service Ceiling - 35,500 ft.
Two 20 m.m. Cannon
Two - 7.7 m.m. Fixed Mach. Guns

IDENTIFICATION POSTER #103
FROM DATA CURRENTLY AVAILABLE
21367A C

Japanese Zero   USAF

Japanese Navy Rufe fighter seaplane, used in the Aleutians.   USAF

167

RCAF IN ALASKA

The United States had too little air strength to protect the vast territory of Alaska and the Aleutians, so when Dutch Harbor was attacked and the Japanese gained a foothold in the Aleutians, Canada was asked to supply air crews and planes. It responded with a bomber reconnaissance squadron to Kodiak and a fighter squadron that flew patrols out of Kodiak, plus trained crews which at times flew U.S. planes with U.S. markings.

When American planes were moved out to the Aleutian Chain the Canadians took over the defense of Anchorage at Elmendorf Field. They too were soon moved down the chain and flew out of Umnak.

In the summer of 1942, the 115th Fighter Squadron occupied the Annette Island airfield and flew patrols over southeastern Alaska and the northern British Columbia coast.

On one field used by the Canadians, a herd of caribou kept all the aircraft grounded. They swarmed over the runways by the hundreds and airmen had to chase them off with shovels.

In August 1942, part of the force moved out to Adak and in 1943 moved forward to Amchitka with P-40 Kittyhawks.[3] The squadrons were organized too late to take part in the Attu campaign but did fly 60 missions over Kiska, including the last Allied strike before the Japanese evacuated the island.[4]

KURILE ISLANDS RAIDS

The Kurile Islands are the northern extension of the Japanese islands and were used as air and naval bases during the war. As American footholds spread west in the Aleutians, U.S. forces had an opportunity to bomb these.[5] Attu, recaptured in May 1943, was only 650 miles from the Kuriles.

The first raid from the Aleutians was on July 18, 1943, when six B-24s raided the bases at Paramushiro. Gen. Butler ordered his 11th Air Force to make a major raid on Sept. 11, 1943. Only eight B-24s and 12 B-25s were available. Sixty enemy fighters were waiting for them and only nine American planes returned. The rest were either shot down or crashed in Soviet Siberia.

[3]The Canadian P-40s were called Kittyhawks instead of the U.S. name, Warhawks.

[4]Canada supplied the following units: 115th Fighter Squadron; 111th Fighter Squadron; #14 Fighter Squadron and the 8th Bomber Recon Squadron (Bolingbrokes).

[5]The Allied Combined Chiefs of Staff had decided in 1943 to build staging bases in the Aleutians for a possible invasion of Japan in 1944. The plan of course was never carried out.

This was to be the last Air Force raid of 1943 from the Aleutians.

On Dec. 20, 1943, however, PBYs from VP-43 made the first night raid on the Kuriles, and became the first Navy aircraft to bomb the Japanese homeland during the war.

The 11th Air Force and Navy PBYs and Ventura bombers moved to the new base on Shemya and spent the last 20 months of the war bombing from there.

More than 1,500 sorties were flown from the Aleutians over the enemy bases on Paramushiro and Shumushu islands of the Kuriles before the last mission on Aug. 13, 1945.[6]

[6]An emergency landing field was available at Petropavlosk on the Soviet's Kamchatka Peninsula but personnel who were forced to land there could be interned because Russia and Japan were not at war.

Map 13
Japanese Kurile Islands.

Brig. Gen. Earl H. DeFord who took over the 11th Bomber Command in January 1943.
USAF

Brig. Gen. William O. Butler, left, commander of the Army Air Force in Alaska with Col. William
O. Eareckson, commander of the 11th Bomber Command in Alaska.   USAF

Bomber pilots receive instructions for a raid on Kiska from Col. Eareckson (bareheaded)
of the 11th Bomber Command.   USAF

Maj. Jack Chennault commanded the 11th Fighter Squadron in the Aleutians. Like his famous father, Claire Chennault of the "Flying Tigers," he had his plane painted with the tiger jaws. FR

A bomb addressed to Japanese Premier Tojo is loaded on a B-24. USAF

Air Force bombers literally blew this 280-foot ship out of the water at a harbor in the Aleutian Islands with a salvo of heavy bombs. The ship snapped apart before sinking. *USAF*

A soldier carries 50-caliber machine gun ammunition to a B-25 bomber. *USAF*

Pilots run to their planes during an alert on Umnak Island in 1942. USA

Pilots and navigators relaxing in the early morning hours waiting to go out on a bombing raid over Kiska from Umnak Island, 1942. USA

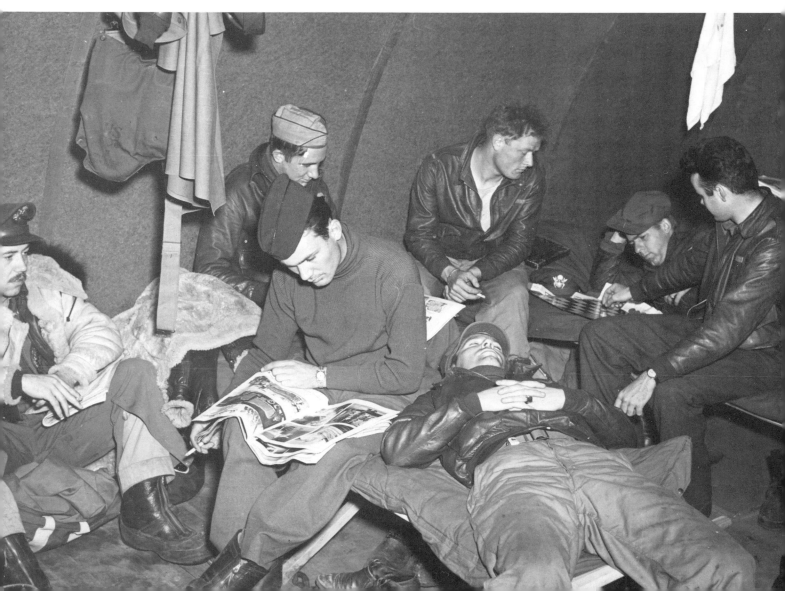

A metal Marston mat is laid over the soggy tundra to provide a firm runway. USA

This structure is the collapsible, sectional steel frame of a canvas airplane hangar at an air base on an Aleutian Island. Covered with pre-sized strips of camouflaged canvas, the hangar could house several small and medium bombers and could be moved to a new location in a few days. NA

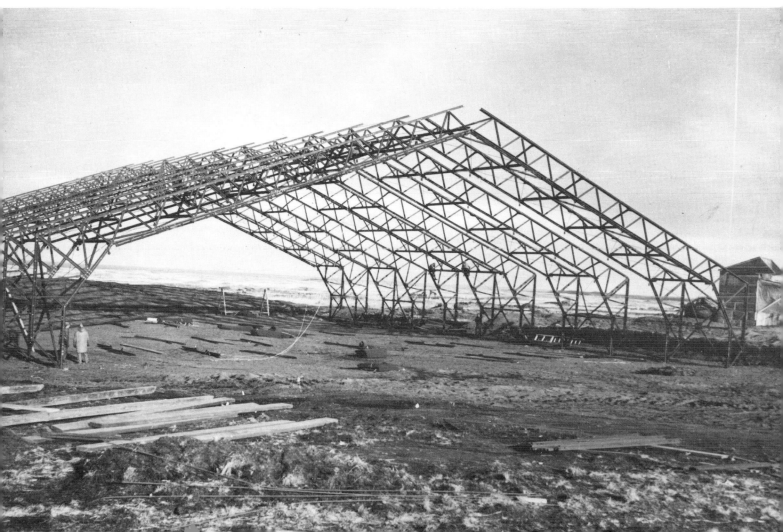

A snowy, soggy Aleutian airfield. *USAF*

The ever-present fog provides a backdrop for P-40s of the 11th Air Force at Alexai Point Airbase on Attu in 1943. *USAF*

The first zero captured intact, its pilot had made a forced landing on Akutan Island after the Dutch Harbor attack and was killed. It was found five weeks later and shipped back to the United States for study. RC

The damaged Zero is hoisted onto the dock at Dutch Harbor for shipment back to the United States.

AHFAM

A damaged B-25 lies partly off the runway at Alexai Point on Attu after striking the tail of another B-25 on Nov. 13, 1943. *USAF*

Unable to land at its home base because of fog, a B-24 Liberator bomber returning from a bombing run has found a landing site in the soggy tundra of a tiny island in the Aleutians. Parts of this plane can still be seen on Great Sitkin Island. *USAF*

An A-20 (left) and B-25 (right) parked in front of the operations building at Ladd Field, near Fairbanks, in February 1944. The temperature was − 35°F.　　　　　　　　　　　　　　　　*USAF*

Aircraft engines being preheated by warm air to save time and prevent engine damage. A small gasoline engine runs fans which drive warm air through the pipes to the engines. The hoods around the engines confine the heat. Engines were thus brought to a proper flying temperature in from 15 minutes to an hour, depending on the temperature. In extreme cold, engines could not be turned over at all unless they were preheated.　　　　　　　　　　　　　　　　*NA*

Several types of aircraft are repaired in a revetment at an Aleutian air base.   USAF

A rubber raft floats beside a C-47 parked on the flooded runway on Adak.   USAF

A P-38 Lightning, one of the deadliest fighter-bombers of the war.   *USAF*

A painting of Lt. Stanley Long's P-38 shooting down a Japanese Mavis Flying Boat over Atka Island on Aug. 4, 1942. It was the first aerial victory for a P-38 in the war.   *AAC*

B-25 Mitchells of the 77th Bomb Squadron, 28th Bomb Group, fly in formation over water southeast of Attu in September 1943.   USAF

Crew of the "Kiska Katie" B-24 bomber on Adak after a bombing run.   USAF

An early-model B-17 named "Old Seventy." It was flown by the 36th Bomb Squadron in its futile attempt to find the Japanese Navy before the attack on Dutch Harbor. On July 17, 1942, with Capt. Jack Marks at the controls, it flew into a fog shrouded mountain after a fight with Rufe fighters. BC

B-17 Flying Fortresses were used in the bombing of Kiska. BC

Canadian Kittyhawks of Number 14 Fighter Squadron at Cape Field on Umnak Island in 1943.   AAC

Inspecting the Canadian Bolingbrook bombers at Yakutat, Alaska in 1942.   RC

Shemya Island before the airfield was built. The house built in 1924 by the Aleutian Fur Company, was used later by the Army Engineers. FR

Aerial view of Shemya Island in October 1943, four months after its occupation by American troops. It became a major base for the bombing of the northern Kurile Islands in 1944-45. USA

A P-39 with extra fuel tanks slung underneath taxis to a runway for takeoff.   USA

C-47s of the Air Transport Command stand on the Shemya runway in late 1944.   USAF

A B-25 Mitchell bomber, right, pulls out of a bomb run over snow-covered Kashiwabara army staging area on Paramushiro Island in the Japanese northern Kurile Islands. It has just strafed troops and buildings after scoring direct hits on a 2,500-ton cargo ship seen exploding and burning in the bay.   USAF

The Japanese turned the village of Paramushiro on Kurile Island into a powerful air base. This 1944 photograph shows (1) hangar, (2) Mt. Suribachi, (3) air strip, (4) revetments, (5) radio station, (6) anti-aircraft emplacements and (7) canneries along the waterfront.   USAF

A tree planted by Russian traders before the sale of Alaska to the United States disputes the geographic truth that no tree grows in the Aleutians west of 160 degrees longitude.

USAF

TREE
ONLY ONE ON
ATTU

THE BATTLE
OF ATTU
19 DAYS OF HELL

After the battle of Dutch Harbor, Japanese forces proceeded to occupy the westernmost islands of the Aleutians--Attu and Kiska. Ultimately, about 8,600 troops were deployed on the two islands.

There were 42 natives on Attu plus Mr. and Mrs. C. Foster Jones, Bureau of Indian Affairs teachers and operators of the island's radio station. The Navy had wanted to evacuate these people in May 1942 but the weather had not permitted it. When the enemy soldiers came into Attu village on June 7, Jones tried to escape to the hills and was gunned down. Mrs. Jones and the natives were held at the village for three months and then were taken to Japan where they were interned until the end of the war. Seventeen of the natives died in captivity.

Gen. Higudu of the Japanese Northern Army said Japan's Aleutian campaign had three objectives: to prevent American use of the chain to mount offensive operations, to drive a wedge between U.S. and Soviet insular possessions, and to establish bases for air operations against Alaska and the west coasts of Canada and the United States. None of these objectives was achieved.

The Japanese established a camp at Holtz Bay on Attu and immediately began to fortify the island. In September, the high command decided to consolidate all troops at Kiska and to speed up work on the airfield there, but then -- because of the U.S. naval blockade in the Aleutians, which was feared to presage an invasion of northern Japan -- reversed the decision and reoccupied Attu.

On Oct. 29, 1942, Japanese troops again set up a camp at Holtz Bay, and on Nov. 7 a break in the weather permitted an American patrol plane to discover that Attu had been reoccupied.

The 11th Air Force bombed Attu and Kiska from Umnak, Adak, and Amchitka, and Navy PBYs continued for a time to attack the islands out of Atka. The bombing strikes were designed largely to interfere with airfield construction, which was difficult enough for the Japanese anyway because of the muskeg conditions and its lack of heavy construction equipment.

Attu village before the war. The weather station-radio tower is in the right foreground. On June 7, 1942, the Japanese stormed ashore and took over the village, killing Charles Jones, the radio operator.   NA

188

By early 1943, Adm. Kinkaid's effective naval blockade and the constant pounding from the air were making the invaders' situation desperate. In the United States, meanwhile, there was a rising clamor for expulsion of the enemy from U.S. territory.

Despite these problems, Imperial Japanese Headquarters decided to keep troops on both islands as a deterrent to a possible American invasion of northern Japan. Several convoys with troops and supplies tried to get through the naval blockade, but most of the ships were either sunk or turned back.

A large convoy did manage to slip through to Attu in the fog on March 9, 1943, and the next day the last supply ship reached the beach. There would be no more troops or supplies to the island. The occupying troops were on their own.

In April, a submarine got into Chichagof Harbor, bringing Col. Yasugo Yamasaki to the unenviable task of commanding the troops. At his disposal were about 2,650 second-rate soldiers, 12 anti-aircraft guns and some coastal artillery. Yamasaki knew it was only a matter of time before the Americans would try to take back the island. Since Attu was too big to cover with his small

forces, he ordered his men into the mountains to build fortifications on the ridges above Massacre and Holtz valleys. His main camp was in the Chichagof Valley.

The Samurai code dictated death or victory for the Japanese. There was no thought of surrender.

The Americans' original idea was to invade Kiska in May and then take Attu, further out on the chain. However, in March, Allied commanders decided to invade Attu first, bypassing Kiska, in the island-hopping technique that was to be used so effectively in the South Pacific. This was an important decision. On Attu the landing force faced about half the 6,000 troops they would have encountered on Kiska.

Since the Army troops then in Alaska were scattered over a wide area, it was necessary to look to the States for a cohesive attack force. The War Department chose the 7th Motorized Division, then training in the California desert for use in the North African campaign, with Maj. Gen. Albert Brown in command. D-Day was set for May 7, 1943.

This would be the U.S. Army's first island amphibious landing of the war and a joint

A captured photograph thought to show Japanese troops landing on Attu on June 7, 1942.

UAA

Alaska staff was sent to San Diego to prepare the division for the rigorous Aleutian campaign.

Optimism ran high, with air and sea superiority, and with 16,000 troops at their disposal, U.S. Commanders believed they could conquer the island in a matter of days.

In retrospect, however, it was clear that this campaign had been mounted too hastily. The Joint Chiefs of Staff wanted to get the enemy out of the Aleutians so that, if Russia entered the war, the islands could be used as a forward base for an invasion of Japan. The troops of the division were ill-prepared for their assignment. When they boarded ship in California, they thought they were going into action in the South Pacific. They were not even issued proper winter clothing.

To the problems of inadequate training, clothing and cold-weather supplies were added substandard maps and intelligence and lack of cooperation and coordination among the various commands. All these were factors in a campaign that was to prove far longer and more costly than had been projected.

The 11th Air Force and Navy PBYs kept up their bomb runs over both Attu and Kiska as invasion time neared. Kiska was attacked as heavily as Attu in an attempt to mislead the defenders.

The invasion fleet[1] consisted of 34 ships, with troops crammed into every available space. The fleet sailed for Attu from Cold Bay on May 4, but because of bad weather, the invasion had to

---

[1]The fleet included the battleships **Nevada, Idaho,** and **Pennsylvania,** the CVE Carrier **Nassau,** plus an assortment of cruisers, destroyers, submarines and four troop transports.

Mr. and Mrs. C. Foster Jones were the only white people living on Attu when the Japanese invaded. Mr. Jones was killed in the attack. Mrs. Jones was captured and taken to Japan for the duration of the war. They were teachers for the Bureau of Indian Affairs and operated the weather radio station.

AHL

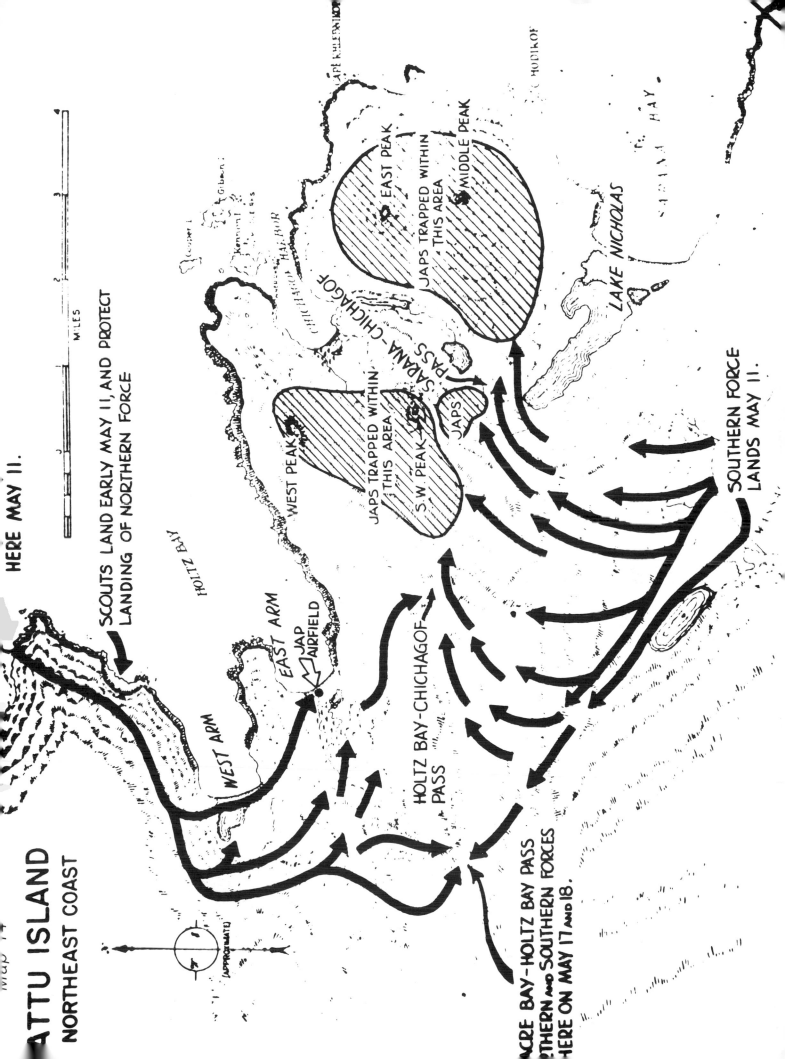

ATTU ISLAND
NORTHEAST COAST

HERE MAY 11.

SCOUTS LAND EARLY MAY 11, AND PROTECT
LANDING OF NORTHERN FORCE

WEST ARM

WEST PEAK

EAST ARM

HOLTZ BAY

JAP
AIRFIELD

JAPS TRAPPED WITHIN
THIS AREA

S.W. PEAK

JAPS

SARANA-CHICHAGOF
PASS

CHICHAGOF HARBOR

EAST PEAK

JAPS TRAPPED WITHIN THIS AREA

MIDDLE PEAK

CAPE KHODIKOF

SARANA BAY

LAKE NICHOLAS

HOLTZ BAY-CHICHAGOF
PASS

SOUTHERN FORCE
LANDS MAY 11.

ACRE BAY-HOLTZ BAY PASS
THERN and SOUTHERN FORCES
HERE ON MAY 17 and 18.

MILES

(APPROXIMATE)

be put off until the morning of May 11.

The Japanese were well dug in at sites around Holtz and Chichagof harbors and were waiting for the Americans to come. The American plan was to land troops above and below the twin enemy encampments. One force would land on the north side of Holtz Bay and push southeast. A second, larger force would land at Massacre Bay[2] to the south and push north. The two forces would then join and make the final push against the enemy around Chichagof Harbor.

Capt. Willoughby's Scout battalion was the first to land at Red Beach on Holtz Bay and immediately started its push south. As the beach was undefended, the rest of the northern force landed within hours. There were steep cliffs in this part of the bay and the enemy had not expected a landing at such an umpromising spot.

To the south troops landed on the beaches of Massacre Bay. Both landings had been in dense fog and were unopposed. It looked as though it would just be a matter of clearing the enemy out of the hills and the battle would be over. But it was to take 19 days and more than 500 American dead to finally secure the island.

Massacre Valley ran north for two miles with a hogback ridge in the middle. The invading troops came under intense fire from the dug-in enemy troops and the battle raged there for five frightful days.

The Alaska Scouts on the north side of the island had packed food for only a couple of days, expecting to meet up with the southern force in short order. After five days the Scouts finally got to the Holtz Bay-Chichagof Pass area, but only six men out of 200 were able to continue the fight.

The Aleutian cold and wet muskeg were putting more men out of action than the enemy.[3]

[2]Massacre Bay was named after Russians had massacred the Aleut natives there in the late 18th century.

[3]Attu's temperatures ranged from freezing point at night to 45 degrees in the daytime. The troops were outfitted with leather boots which could not keep out the ever present water from the muskeg. Thus hundreds got "immersion foot" with the same effects as associated with frost-bitten feet.

In the pilot house of the **U.S.S. Casco** *off Chichagof Harbor. Left to right: Mike Hodakof, Chief of the Aleuts;* **Casco's** *officer-of-the-deck; Commander Theda Combs, Commanding Officer of the* **Casco;** *and Lieut. Comm. C. E. Squeaky Anderson, the beach commander.* RC

Since wheeled transport was useless in the muskeg, many combat troops had to be taken from the front and put to work carrying supplies by hand for miles through the cold muskeg and snow.

Due to problems between the High Command and Gen. Brown, Adm. Kinkaid relieved him of command and replaced him with Gen. Eugene Landrum, after six days of battle. Two days later, troops of Alaska's 4th Infantry Regiment stormed ashore to help the beleaguered 7th Division. There were now 16,000 Americans on the island trying to dislodge the approximate 1,500 remaining Japanese troops.

As weather conditions improved, planes got through to bomb enemy positions. The Japanese tried several times to bring in their own bombers, but these were either shot down or driven off. Ships offshore added their batteries to the firepower battering the Japanese.

After two weeks of fighting, American forces had pushed the enemy back into the Chichagof Valley. Only two prisoners had been taken.

Col. Yamasaki's position had now become desperate. There was no thought of being rescued by ship. The only hope of the Japanese was to storm the American positions to get to their food and seize the ammunition dumps in Massacre Valley. It was a wild gamble at best.

On the morning of May 29, nineteen days after the start of the battle, Yamasaki's men, 800 in all, attacked the American lines between Fishhook Ridge and Buffalo Ridge.[4] They overran the American positions, and stormed up Engineer Hill inflicting heavy casualties on the U.S. forces. At the crest of the hill, Gen. Archibald Arnold had gathered all available men -- cooks, medics, engineers and anyone else who could shoulder a rifle -- and stopped the Japanese attack. The enemy tried several more scattered assaults, but had lost its strength. Before the end of the day, 500 Japanese committed suicide rather than surrender. Col. Yamasaki himself was killed in the last attack of the day.

By May 30 the battle was over, although it took nearly three more months to flush the last enemy from the hills. In all 549 Americans were killed, and more than 3,200 were wounded or suffered from exposure or other battle injuries. Of the approximate 2,600 Japanese troops on the island only 28 were taken prisoner. All others had honored the Samurai code of death.

---

[4]Over 600 wounded Japanese were killed by their own men rather than surrender to the Americans on May 28 before the last attack up Engineer Hill.

Col. Benjamin Talley's engineers unloaded their construction equipment while the battle raged and began building an airfield for the coming invasion of Kiska. It was ready for use by June 8, accommodating PBYs and land-based Ventura bombers as well as Air Force planes.

The Japanese High Command acknowledged the loss of Attu and made plans to extradite itself from Kiska without loss of face. On May 30 it issued this final communique on Attu: "The Japanese garrison on the island of Attu has been conducting a bloody battle with a small number of troops against a numerically far superior enemy under many difficulties, and on the night of May 29 carried out an heroic assault against the main body of enemy invaders with the determination to inflict a final blow on them and display the true spirit of the Imperial Army.

"Since then there has been no communication from the Japanese forces on the island and it is now estimated that the entire Japanese force has preferred death to dishonor."

"Along with three or four enlisted men, we were the Aleutian Section of G-2. Although I had no formal instruction in aerial photo reading or interpretation, I proposed the estimates of enemy forces for the attacks on both Attu and Kiska, mostly from aerial photos of those and some adjacent islands, augmented by visual observation as reported by pilots of aircraft returning from missions over these islands.

"My boss, a well qualified officer who had lived in Japan and served there as a military attache, revised downward my estimate of enemy forces on Attu. Even though he cut my estimate by about 30%, it still was far more accurate than most estimates I saw later in Europe.

"It was estimated that there were 75 to 125 Japanese troops on Attu. I estimated 2,250 to 2,500. My boss cut the estimate to about 1,500-1,800. When the last Japanese was killed or captured, the count was either 2,249 or 2,251.

"As a result of my good estimate (even after being reduced downward) I was sent to the Kiska operations as the official War Department observer.

"Although I personally believed there were about 7,200 Japanese on Kiska, I did raise my formal estimate to 8,000 to please my superior who by this time believed there really were enemy forces in the Aleutians.

"My estimate of enemy forces was based on three general factors: tentage and buildings believed to be used for personal shelter; estimated size and caliber, location and type of weapons and probable organization. It finally summed up, after several months of observation that for every four artillery pieces in an area, there was a battery of 250 soldiers. That is why my personal estimate was 2,250-2,500 on Attu."

Tom Boardman
Boise, Idaho

A cable hauls supplies and tractors onto the ridge between Red Beach and Holtz Bay. At the base of the cliff is the supply dump where a Jeep is being made fast to be pulled up the incline.

USA

General view of landing operations. Ships are lying off the beach and tents of the landed troops are in the background. Some vehicles and troops have started to push forward.

NA

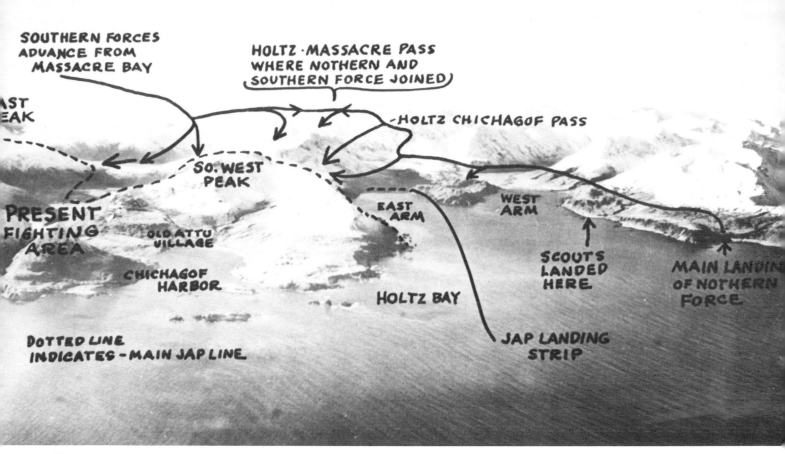

The initial American landing on Attu and subsequent battle positions.   UAA

Maj. Gen. A. M. Landrum, left, talks to Brig. Gen. Archibald V. Arnold, right.   USA

A tent city rises on the shores of Attu. Landing boats are bringing in more supplies.
NA

The first flag to fly over Attu was erected on the deck of an abandoned Japanese landing boat on the beach.
USA

A vehicle and equipment bog down in mud.

USA

Troops fighting in the Chichagof area were supplied by hand because the terrain made the use of vehicles impossible. A supply dump is in the middle of the picture. This pass is between the East Arm of Holtz Bay and Chichagof Bay.

USA

A field hospital stands at the foot of the ridge at Red Beach. Two of the tents were used for surgery the other two for wards. The holes in the hillside are foxholes dug by soldiers for protection at night.

USA

While their comrades move forward, troops curl up to rest in sleeping bags behind an earthen barricade.

NA

Looking southeast from about 5,000 yards inland, from the beach. A Japanese camp was located in the valley. On the left is a barracks that had been burned by the Japanese when they were forced to evacuate the area. Next to the burned barracks is a wooden supply building camouflaged with tundra and dirt. On the plateau above, about 15 wooden barracks were built in the ground and covered with tundra and dirt. In the rear of the plateau, to the left of the aerial poles, was a radio station. The ground under the camp was honeycombed with tunnels and other large rooms, the entrances of which can be seen in the sides of the hills.   USA

General view on May 13 of the top of the ridge between Red Beach, where the American forces landed, and Holtz Bay. This picture shows the battle area occupied by the troops while they were trying to dislodge Japanese forces from the bay area. The battalion command post was located at the radio antenna seen in the middle foreground.   USA

Troops do their laundry during a lull in the fighting.

USA

Gen. S. B. Buckner talks to officers on an inspection tour of Attu during the last phase of the battle.

USA

Medics massage the frozen feet of a soldier who spent 24 hours under fire in a water-filled trench. Cold caused more casualties than the Japanese. *USA*

Looking northwest from atop the ridge between Holtz Bay and Chichagof Bay, showing the complete Holtz Bay Area. In the foreground can be seen a Japanese Zero which had been shot down or crashed early in the spring. To the front and slightly to the right of the plane men are unloading supplies from landing barges. On the first rise above the beach the Japanese had located a battery of six anti-aircraft and artillery guns. Ahead of these guns they had dug several long trenches for riflemen and machine guns. On the hill directly behind the gun emplacements were caves for the storing of ammunition and rations. On top of the second rise were other trenches and some caves for living quarters. *USA*

American soldiers show off captured Japanese equipment on Attu.   USAF

A captured Japanese photograph shows U.S. artillery fire at Chichagof Harbor.   USAF

A pushcart railway built by the Japanese. The carts were constructed so as to be either flat cars or hoppers when the sides, which the carts are leaning against, were put in position. USA

Japanese dead litter the battlefield near Chichagof Harbor. Some committed "hara-kari," some were killed by the American troops. USA

Japanese 70-mm gun captured on Attu.

USA

Interior of a Japanese conical tent after its capture. Most of the mess was made by American troops looking for souvenirs.

USA

A dummy Japanese anti-aircraft gun on Attu.

Thomas Pynn
St. Petersburg, Florida

In the last days of the battle several prisoners were taken. The prisoner is showing enemy
pontoons to the G2 staff.

Thomas Pynn
St. Petersburg, Florida

Canadian and American flags fly atop the highest point on Red Beach at the northern tip of the island on Aug. 16. Men are still unloading barges on the beach.   USA

THE KISKA OCCUPATION
WHAT HAPPENED TO THE ENEMY?

With the battle of Attu over, American commanders turned to the problem of expelling the Japanese from Kiska with a minimum of casualties and without the mistakes made on Attu.

Early in July 1942, the Japanese reinforced Kiska with 1,200 additional men and six midget submarines.[1] This brought the force up to 2,450 officers and men. Eighteen float planes were based in Kiska Harbor in June, but by August only two had not been shot down or destroyed in the water. Six Mavis bombers were also brought in to try to counter the growing American air power. Two were shot down over Atka on Aug. 4 by newly arrived P-38 fighters, the first kills of the war for the P-38.

With American air and naval power gaining the upper hand, it became increasingly difficult for the Japanese to supply the garrison. An airfield on the island was a necessity, but heavy construction equipment was needed to build a field on the muskeg.[2] Since the only safe way was to resupply by submarine, heavy equipment could not be brought in. The field had to be built by hard and time-consuming hand labor.

The Japanese were successful at concentrating a tremendous number of anti-aircraft batteries around Kiska Harbor, and these played havoc with low-level bomb runs. They did not stop American planes from bombing whenever the weather conditions permitted, however.

On July 18, a little over a month after the occupation of Kiska, Adm. Theobald took his fleet of five cruisers and nine destroyers to Kiska to try to dislodge the invaders by naval gunfire. The weather was so bad that he never got close enough to fire his guns and four destroyers were damaged by collisions in the fog. He turned back disgusted at the whole affair.

On Aug. 3 he sent the fleet out again with Rear Adm. William "Poco" Smith in command. The weather was better and Smith got to the island. His observation planes could not see the targets because of smoke from the anti-aircraft batteries, however, so the fleet bombarded the island blindly, causing little damage.

With the action in far-off Guadalcanal heating up in the first part of August, Adm. Nimitz had to recall part of Theobald's fleet to the South Pacific.

Thus 1942 ended with the Navy and the Japanese at a standoff.

By the middle of 1943, with the Attu garrison annihilated, the Japanese on Kiska really had no hope of being reinforced or of stopping the expected invasion. American air supremacy and the naval blockade had seen to this. Their only hope now was in being evacuated before the Americans came.

All through May, June, July, and early August 1943, the 11th Air Force continued its bombing of enemy installations on Kiska. Planes flew from bases on newly captured Attu, Shemya, Amchitka, and Adak. There was good weather in July and with 16 hours of daylight, planes could bomb around the clock. The 11th had close to 350 combat planes, the greatest concentration of the Aleutian campaign. These planes dropped more than 300,000 pounds of explosives on one day alone--Aug. 4. Despite this, heavy anti-aircraft fire continued.

The Navy, too, was active. With several major battleships and many cruisers and destroyers, it kept up a bombing pattern of its own for several weeks before the invasion.

Enemy troop strength on Kiska had been estimated at as high as 9,000. Allied commanders were not going to take any chances with a force this big. There had been too many casualties on Attu.

The invasion of Kiska, code named **Operation Cottage,** took place on Aug. 15, 1943. Maj. Gen. Charles Corlett commanded the invasion force. He had at his disposal 15,000 troops of the 7th Division, some of them veterans of Attu; 5,000 troops of the 87th Mountain Combat Team, trained for mountain fighting; 5,300 troops of the 13th Royal Canadian Infantry Brigade; and 2,500 American and Canadian members of the 1st Special Service Force, a highly trained unit of paratroopers and amphibious troops.[3] Total troop strength was more than 34,000 men, a formidable force to send against the well dug-in enemy troops.

Troops were trained on Adak and Amchitka for the upcoming battle. Casualties were expected to be high even with the massive pre-invasion bombardment.

Military planners in Japan wanted to get their troops off Kiska. They had already given up any hope of keeping a toehold in the Aleutians. They could use these troops more effectively elsewhere. With the ring of steel surrounding the island, thrown up by the U.S. Navy, the only possible way

---

[1]There were a few troops on Agattu Island but they were brought back to Kiska.

[2]The Japanese mechanized equipment amounted to 60 trucks, 14 cars, 20 motorcycles and two tractors.

[3]Troops of the 1st Special Service Force and the Alaska Scouts were the first ashore at Gertrude Cove on the southwest end of the island.

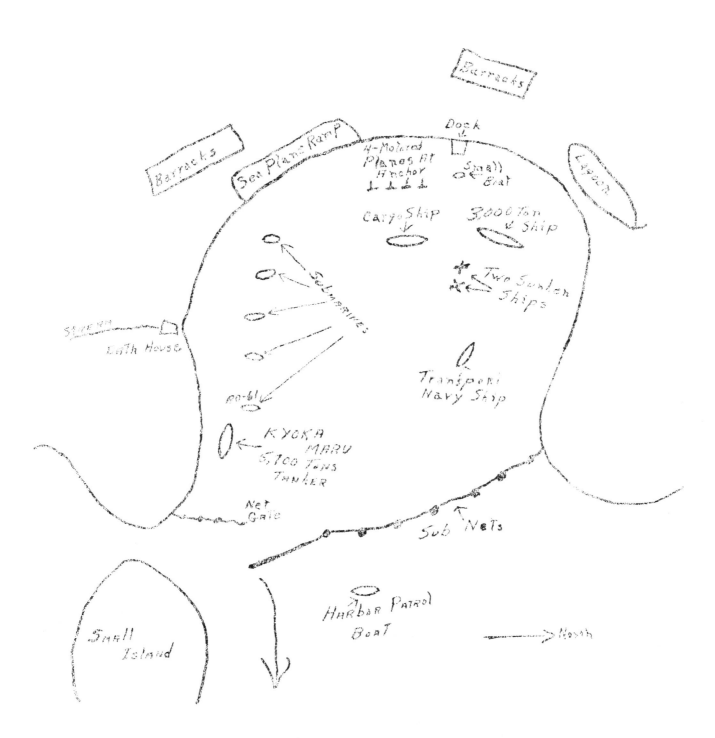

Map 15
A captured Japanese Navy torpedoman drew this detailed map of Kiska Harbor in September 1942.   NA

to evacuate what proved to be 6,000 troops was by submarine.[4] Several I-class submarines got in and took some of the men off, but they were too small to evacuate the whole island. Several were sunk by American planes. Another way had to be found.

By mid-July, with the American bombing and shelling reaching an intolerable state, Adm. Kawase, commander of Japanese naval forces in the North Pacific, was given a bold plan. A fleet of destroyers would steam into Kiska Harbor under cover of fog, quickly load the troops and race back to their home territory.

Day by day the plight of the Japanese troops was getting more desperate. Food was short and the daily bombing forced them to hole up in their underground bunkers. They knew that any day the Americans would come, and their fate would be the same as that of their brothers on Attu.

The evacuation fleet of three cruisers and 11 destroyers left Paramushiro in the Kurile Islands on July 21, 1943. They would wait for fog, dash

[4]Additional troops were moved from Attu in September 1942 and more landed on Nov. 8, 1942.

into Kiska Harbor, pick up the men and steam for home. Before noon on July 28, Kawase's fleet was within 50 miles of Kiska. He had lost two of his destroyers in a collision due to fog, but nine destroyers dashed in and evacuated the remaining 5,300 men waiting on the beach. Fog had not reduced visibility to zero, but Kawase could not wait any longer to go in. The destroyers slipped by the Americans on the way out and arrived at their home base on Aug. 1.

The American fleet had left the gate to Kiska open the day before as most of the blockade fleet was off fighting the supposed enemy in the Battle of the Pips. Ships had to refuel and rearm and they had to leave their battle stations at Kiska to do it. This afforded the Japanese their one chance to get into the harbor.

The aerial and naval bombardment of the island continued until the day of the invasion. The Americans suspected that there had been an evacuation, but they were taking no chances. After July 28 there was no more flak from the anti-aircraft batteries, and aerial photos showed no sign of life on the island. If in fact the enemy

Men of the weather detachment on Kiska, May 1942. All were taken prisoner by Japanese troops on June 7, 1942, except men standing 4th and 6th from left.
Left to right standing: Turner, Coefield, House, Mull, Echols, Yaconelli and Coeurtnay.
Left to right front: McCandless, Christiansen, Winfrey with Explosion, Palmer and Gaffey. RC

210

had left, the invasion would be good practice. If the enemy had retreated into caves in the hills to wait for the invasion, there would be a much superior force to deal with them. Either way this action would put an end to enemy occupation of United States territory.

When American and Canadian forces stormed ashore on Aug. 15, all they found were a few dogs and a massive enemy underground defense system.[5]

Military and personal gear of every description, including a British naval gun captured at Singapore, was found abandoned.

Although there were no enemy troops on the island, 24 men were killed by their comrades in the darkness and four died from booby traps left by the Japanese. Fifty others were wounded.

In an island cove, the destroyer, **U.S.S. Abner Read** was damaged by a Japanese mine with the loss of 71 men. Twenty-four others were injured.

---

[5]The dog Explosion had been left on the island when the Japanese occupied it and met the Americans as they waded ashore.

It took another few days to secure the island and make sure no enemy troops were left. Most of the troops left shortly afterward, but the Canadians stayed on for occupation duty for four months.

A lot of flak was produced in official quarters over the fact that the Japanese had slipped through the blockade. But no matter how the enemy got off the island, they were gone with a minimum amount of casualties.

Thus ended active combat in the Aleutians. Although the Japanese had lost their foothold in the islands, they had used a few thousand troops to tie up close to half a million Allied troops for almost a year and a half.

After the Kiska invasion, the war wound down. Alaska was free of the enemy and the troops stationed there were needed elsewhere. Buckner wanted to use the islands as a springboard for a northern invasion route to Japan. Several things prevented this.

Russia had not entered the war against Japan, and without her the invasion route would not be

"Bombs away" on the Kiska installations. One bomb has exploded to the right of the seaplane ramp and several more are falling at the bottom right of the photograph. USAF

211

secure. The bad weather in this part of the world precluded its use as a dependable line of supply for any invasion. Allied forces were already working their way to Japan by the island-hopping process.

Thousands of troops were moved south, fighters and bombers went to other war zones and most ships went to the South Pacific.

Gen. Buckner left in June 1944 to take over command of the 10th Army for its final drive to Japan.[6] His successor was Maj. Gen. Davenport Johnson. He had a tough job--stepping into Buckner's shoes and trying to maintain morale among the remaining troops. The major problem was the lack of anything for the troops to do.

[6]Buckner was killed at the Battle of Okinawa on June 18, 1945 leading the Tenth Army.

The closest enemy force was 650 miles away in the Kurile Islands, and it did not have the desire or strength to bother this part of the world again.

Scores of Hollywood personalities came north to cheer the troops. Better housing and recreational facilities were built. President Roosevelt visited the area in August 1944, and congressional committees dropped in from time to time. But for the most part this area was forgotten, bypassed by action farther south.

The Joint Chiefs in Washington wanted to keep Buckner's northern invasion plans active, but without Soviet help they would not work. The continued presence of land, sea and air forces in the Aleutians did, however, tie up thousands of Japanese forces until the end of the war.

Members of the 1st Special Service Force, trained in amphibious landings, prepare for their invasion in advance of the main body in the early morning hours of Aug. 15, 1943.   USA

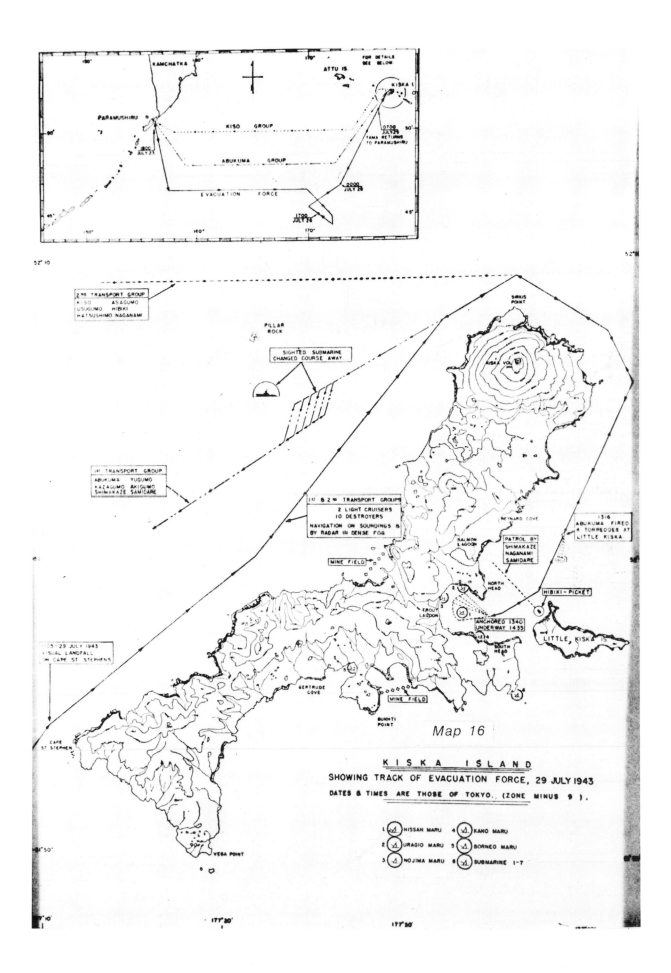

FOR DETAILS
SEE BELOW

2ND TRANSPORT GROUP
KISO   ASAGUMO
USUGUMO   HIBIKI
HATSUSHIMO NAGANAMI

PILLAR
ROCK

SIGHTED SUBMARINE
CHANGED COURSE AWAY

1ST TRANSPORT GROUP
ABUKUMA   YUGUMO
KAZAGUMO AKIGUMO
SHIMAKAZE SAMIDARE

SIRIUS
POINT

KISKA VOL

1ST & 2ND TRANSPORT GROUPS
2 LIGHT CRUISERS
10 DESTROYERS
NAVIGATION ON SOUNDINGS &
BY RADAR IN DENSE FOG

REYNARD COVE

1316
ABUKUMA FIRED
4 TORPEDOES AT
LITTLE KISKA.

PATROL BY
SHIMAKAZE
NAGANAMI
SAMIDARE

SALMON
LAGOON

MINE FIELD

NORTH
HEAD

TROUT
LAGOON

HIBIKI - PICKET

ANCHORED 1340
UNDERWAY 1435

LITTLE KISKA IS.

1105·29 JULY 1943
VISUAL LANDFALL
ON CAPE ST STEPHENS

SOUTH
HEAD

GERTRUDE
COVE

MINE FIELD

BUKHTI
POINT

Map 16

CAPE
ST STEPHEN

KISKA ISLAND

SHOWING TRACK OF EVACUATION FORCE, 29 JULY 1943

DATES & TIMES ARE THOSE OF TOKYO. (ZONE MINUS 9).

VEGA POINT

1 NISSAN MARU   4 KANO MARU
2 URAGIO MARU   5 BORNEO MARU
3 NOJIMA MARU   6 SUBMARINE I-7

KAMCHATKA   ATTU IS.   KISKA I

PARAMUSHIRU

KISO   GROUP

0700
JULY 29
TAMA RETURNS
TO PARAMUSHIRU

1800
JULY 23

ABUKUMA   GROUP

0000
JULY 26

EVACUATION   FORCE

1700
JULY 24

An official Air Force aerial photograph of the Kiska defenses taken in July 1943. Many bomb craters can be seen around the installations.

Robert Durkee
Helena, Montana

An aerial photograph taken on July 22, 1943, shows the rugged volcanic terrain of Kiska and the spit over which the 1st Special Service Force landed. The Kiska volcano slopes upward to the left on the north end of the island.

Robert Durkee
Helena, Montana

A Japanese photograph captured on Guam shows Kiska Harbor and a PBY attacking an enemy transport. The caption read: "12 June 1942, at about 09:10, enemy PBY flying boat receiving intense a/a fire."

Rear Adm. Carrol Jones
Coronado, California

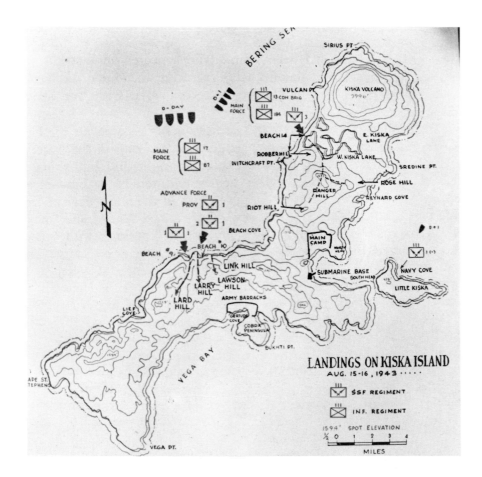

Map 17
Landings on Kiska Island .Aug. 15-16, 1943.

Robert Durkee
Helena, Montana

An aerial view of Kiska harbor showing the seaplane ramp, buildings and seaplanes.   USAF

A photograph made by an 11th Air Force bomber showing the seaplane ramp and buildings.
USAF

LCPs filled with Canadian and American amphibious troops speed awy from Navy transports in their approach to Beaches 9 and 10 during initial landings on Kiska, Aug. 15, 1943.
NA

Staff officers motor in to direct operations of the first wave of attacking troops on Beaches 9 and 10.
NA

Large LSTs are unloaded at Kiska Harbor on Aug. 23. USA

A gunner from the 785th Battery, Royal Canadian Artillery, ignores the sign put up by beach-master Squeaky Anderson. USA

The second landings took place on Aug. 16 on the northern tip of the island near Kiska volcano on Red Beach.
USA

By September the island was bulging with tons of supplies brought ashore for the occupying forces. This is a food and ammunition dump.
USA

ROAD TO MAIN CAMP AND
NORTH CENTRAL KISKA

TANK BARRIER

N.W. END OF RUNWAY

DUMP CAR TRACKS

...ANE REVETMENT

PERIMETER ROADWA...

The northwest end of the Kiska runway. In the left foreground is a completed revetment. Tracks for dump cars used in the construction of the runway are visible. Bomb bursts dot either side of the road leading to the main enemy camp. The angling wall in the distance to the right of the road is a tank barrier.   USAF

The American flag flies over Kiska Harbor in December 1943.   USA

The 24th Field Regiment of the Royal Canadian Artillery passes in review before American officers on Oct. 10, 1943.   USA

Graves of the four Canadians who died by accident during the Kiska Campaign.   USA

The "Nozima Maru," a Japanese merchant ship, lies beached and bombed in Kiska Harbor.

USA

A 75-mm gun emplacement found near Kiska Harbor.

USA

Destroyed midget enemy submarines are examined by Allied personnel.　　　USA

An enemy aircraft hangar destroyed by a direct bomb hit.　　　USA

Lumber stored at the new pier at Kiska Harbor in October 1943.   USA

Lt. Fred Toomoth's dog poses for his master at a party held for men of the 196th Signal
Photo Company on Kiska on Dec. 24, 1943.   USA

Japanese planes and oil and gas drums, wrecked by the incessant aerial bombardments prior to the occupation of Kiska.   USAF

Stockpile of ammunition left by the Japanese when they evacuated Kiska.   USAF

A sign erected by the Japanese at the grave of an American pilot who crashed on Kiska on July 25, 1943, reads: "Sleeping here a brave air-hero Who lost youth and happiness for his Mother land July 25 Nippon army." USAF

A captured Japanese flag displayed by the Kiska occupation force. AAC

Remains of Japanese military equipment and installations on Kiska after the occupation.

Thomas Boardman
Boise, Idaho

Remains of Japanese military equipment and installations on Kiska after the occupation.

Thomas Boardman
Boise, Idaho

Remains of Japanese military equipment and installations on Kiska after the occupation.

Thomas Boardman
Boise, Idaho

Remains of Japanese military equipment and installations on Kiska after the occupation. *Thomas Pynn*
St. Petersburg, Florida

Vehicle remains at Fort Glenn on Umnak Island.

COE

LEGACY OF
THE WAR
LEFTOVERS OF BATTLE

The end of the war in August 1945 brought with it a great sense of relief in Alaska and the entire world. The Japanese menace in Alaska diminished considerably after the reoccupation of Kiska Island in August 1943 and with the ebb of battle forcing the Axis back on all fronts, the war became less and less of a threat to the area.

Since Pearl Harbor, the North Country had been on a war footing although the great distances involved made events happen more slowly than in other theaters of war.

With the conflict over, stock was taken of what the war meant to the country. No longer was this part of North America isolated as it formerly was. There was now a land route connecting the lower 48 states through Canada to Alaska. Many air routes were established which were to be taken over by civilian airlines after the war. Massive airbases, dock facilities, army bases, pipelines, roads, etc. had been constructed for the war against Japan which now lay deserted. Thousands and thousands of soldiers, sailors and airmen and civilian workers had passed through in the past five years and some would doubtless want to return. Natural resources exploration had been expanded and was now needed to fuel the peace-time economy.

The country had awakened, not on its own, but by the sword of the aggresor. Had it not been for the war, it would be conjecture as to how long it would have taken for the modern highways, air routes and construction projects to have been built. Perhaps 40 years later the North Country would still be a sleeping giant known mainly to the rugged individualist and native people who had developed the country up to the beginning of the war.

Material of the vast war machine in 1945 was scattered all the way from Attu in the far Aleutian Chain to the interior of the Northwest Territories in Canada. The quantities of equipment and material were there but there was no use for it.

Hundreds of vehicles of every description littered the Alaska Highway and Canol road. The Aleutian Islands could have literally sunk under the burden of equipment and supplies.

In their haste to leave Kiska the Japanese had abandoned all their war materiel and equipment. Midget submarines were still in their berths and bombed ships littered the harbor. Attu was burdened with the tons of bomb fragments used to dislodge the enemy from the island as was Kiska. Back up the chain all the way to the Alaska Peninsula, war materiel and construction equipment was piled up on dozens of islands.[1]

Several attempts have been made to clean up some of the debris on the islands but the cost and transportation difficulties were prohibitive. The debris on the islands consists of everything from Quonset huts, hangars, runways, cable, submarine nets, barbed wire, 55-gallon steel drums, ammo dumps, aircraft, ships, artillery pieces, pipe, landing mat, radio stations, to bedsprings.[2]

Along the Alaska Highway and Canol road, vehicles and material were bulldozed into pits or similarly destroyed. Some of the equipment was used to keep the highway open in later years. It would have been too great a burden on the Canadian economy to turn over all the equipment to them.

The Canol road was closed in the Northwest Territories and today one can drive the road from Johnsons Crossing to Macmillan Pass with one tourist stop at Ross River. The debris along the road was gradually salvaged and recently the remaining vehicle remains have been gathered in central dumps at Johnsons Crossing, Ross River and near Macmillan Pass.

By October 1947, two American firms had purchased the pipeline for $700,000 and dismantled it. Imperial Oil bought the Whitehorse refinery for $1,000,000 in 1947 and moved it to its more productive oil fields in Alberta.

The Alaska Highway was turned over to the Canadian authorities in April 1946. There was only a small work force to oversee the 1,200 miles of road in Canada. There was an immediate need to upgrade the road and bridges, as there was pressure to open the road to civilian use.

Civilian traffic was restricted in 1946 and 1947. The road was opened for a time in 1948, but had to close because of the high number of car breakdowns. By 1949 the highway was opened on a full-time basis with tourist facilities being expanded every year thereafter. April 1, 1964 saw the highway's military administration come to an end and the Department of Public Works took over the Canadian portion of the road. The Alaska portion is maintained today by the state. This wartime construction project probably

---

[1] Lyman Woodman in his article for the NORTHERN ENGINEER, Vol. 11, No. 4, "Cleaning Up After a War," stated that a recent Draft Environmental Impact Statement offered three possible disposal solutions each costing millions of dollars. On 14 of 28 proposed cleanup sites there was an estimated 6,100 Quonset and Pacific huts, 2,100 wood frame buildings and 20,000 POL (petroleum, oil, lubricants) drums.

[2] **Ibid.**

did more to open up this part of North America than any other during the period.

The wartime boom towns of Dawson Creek, Fort St. John, Fort Nelson, Watson Lake, Whitehorse, Fairbanks and Anchorage have all developed into modern cities, each important in its area as a center of finance, commerce, industry and tourism.

Most of the airfields have been turned over or back to civilian control and there is an excellent string of major and minor airfields throughout the country. The seaplane base at Sitka has been turned into an Indian school and Coast Guard station, the naval base at Kodiak is now a Coast Guard station.

Both pre-war railroads, the Alaska and the White Pass and Yukon, continue to be important links to the interiors of Alaska and Yukon. Whittier was turned over to the Alaska Railroad in 1945, closed in 1946 and again taken over by the Army in August 1946. In 1948 several large concrete buildings were built and the Army maintained the port until it was closed in 1960. Today Whittier has become an important cargo and ferry terminal for southern Alaska.

After the war, the military establishment was greatly reduced but maintained a presence in Alaska. With world tensions again on the rise in the 1950s, Alaska once again took on important defense responsibilities.

At present the one army unit in Alaska is the 172nd Infantry Brigade (Alaska) organized in 1975. When the Air Force was organized from the old Army Air Forces in 1947, Elmendorf Field was turned over to the new organization in 1950 and the Army constructed a new Fort Richardson at its present site near Anchorage. On Jan. 1, 1961 Ladd Field was transferred to the Army and renamed Fort Jonathan M. Wainwright.[3] The Air Force built a new facility at the Old Mile

26 base near Fairbanks and renamed it Eielson Air Force Base.[4]

The Air Transport Command field near Big Delta that had been called Station 17, ATC during the war was reactivated in 1948. It is now called the U.S. Army Cold Region Test Center at Fort Greely.

Naval presence in Alaska is concentrated at the large naval air station on Adak in the Aleutians. It was turned over to the Navy by the Air Force in July 1950. A detachment of P-3 "Orion" patrol aircraft is based there flying anti-submarine patrols, ice patrols, search and rescue missions and routine surveillance flights. The harbor at Sweeper Cove provides full service for naval ships, Coast Guard cutters and State of Alaska craft.

Shemya Airbase was abandoned in 1951 but leased to Northwest Airlines as a refueling stop. The Air Force took over the island again in 1958 and it is now an important defense installation. Kiska was vacated at the end of the war and Attu in 1949. The Coast Guard still maintains a 30-man LORAN station there. Dutch Harbor was abandoned as a naval base and put up as surplus property. Amchitka was abandoned in 1950 and became a site for underground nuclear testing in the 1960s.

Atka village, destroyed in 1942, was rebuilt after the war by the natives.

All but seven of the islands today comprise the Aleutian Islands National Wildlife Refuge with headquarters at Adak. The refuge was established in 1913 by Executive order of President William Howard Taft.

Although the development of the North Country was certainly spurred on tremendously by the war, let us hope that future generations can develop the area by more peaceful means.

[4]Named for Carl Ben Eielson, early Alaska aviation pioneer.

[3]Named for General Jonathan Wainwright who surrendered American forces in the Philippines in May 1942.

This rock cairn was erected in 1946 at the former U.S. Army camp on Acropolis Hill above Prince Rupert B.C. The area has been renamed Roosevelt Park.

Phylis Bowman
Prince Rupert, B.C.

-V-E Day celebration on a baseball field in Whitehorse, May 8, 1945.   USA

V-J Day parade at Edmonton, Alberta, Aug. 15, 1945.   PAA

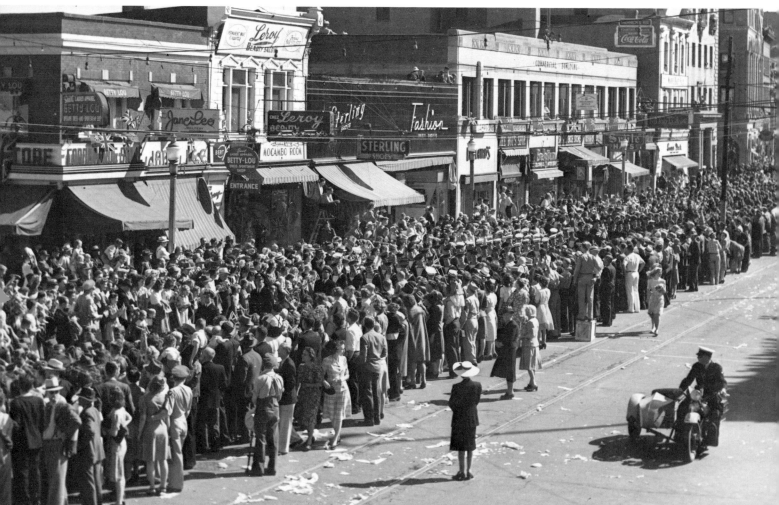

V. J. Day parade down Third Avenue, Prince Rupert, British Columbia on August 15, 1945. Over 1500 troops marched in the parade.

Phylis Bowman
Prince Rupert, B.C.

Port Chilkoot, formerly Chilkoot Barracks, at Haines, Alaska, was bought by a group of veterans in 1947 and turned into a commercial enterprise.

State of Alaska

Some of the vast array of equipment stored on Adak Island in Sept. 1945. The equipment on the Aleutian Islands at the end of the war was left to disintegrate, destroyed on the site or shipped back to the States.   *USA*

Shigeru Inadu, third secretary of the Japanese Embassy in Washington, and other personnel look at the grave of some 40 Japanese war dead who had been disinterred, cremated and reburied. This was done in June 1953 at the Fort Richardson cemetery, where the unknown Japanese soldiers had lain since 1947. They were killed in action on the Aleutian chain and later their bodies were transported to the mainland. The Japanese government requested that the bodies be exhumed for proper Shinto services, including cremation.   *USAF*

HERE LIE
UNIDENTIFIED
JAPANESE SOLDIERS

Surplus trucks and jeeps on the beach at Shemya Island after the war.　　　　*USAF*

Residents of Attu Island waiting for transportation back to their home in April 1945. They had been evacuated from the island more than two years before.　　　*USA*

At the end of the war, Excursion Inlet, which had been built as a port of debarkation for the Attu invasion but never used, was demolished. *USA*

German prisoners of war were used to demolish Excursion Inlet in late 1945. *USA*

Contact Creek at MP 588.1 (Km 946.3) on the Alaska Highway in British Columbia. Construction equipment coming from East and West met here on Sept. 24, 1942. SC

Delta Junction, Alaska, where the Alaska Highway connects with the Richardson Highway. SC

The Sikanni Chief bridge, built in 1943, is still standing at MP 161.5 (Km 259.9) over the Sikanni Chief River, but is no longer used on the highway. This is the same bridge as shown on page 28.   SC

The only original 1942 log bridge still standing on the Alaska Highway is at Canyon Creek, Yukon, MP 996.8 (Km 1604.2).   SC

Remains of a pumping station just north of White Pass in British Columbia along the White Pass and Yukon Route right-of-way. The station was one of several built during the war to pump fuel from Skagway to Whitehorse through a four-inch pipeline. SC

Fuel tanks at the north end of Skagway. They were built during the war and are still in use.
SC

Abandoned trucks left over from the Canol construction project are piled up at the Johnsons Crossing dump. YA

The famous Watson Lake signposts along the Alaska Highway SC

In 1948 these huge apartment and office buildings were built by the Army for use in Whittier. The port was administered by the Army until it was closed in 1960. It now handles civilian traffic and cargo.   AHFAM

The last engine of the ten that were shipped north in 1943 for use on the White Pass and Yukon Route rests beside the Skagway Museum.   DP

Crashed Ventura bomber on Agattu Island.   COE

Remains of a P-38 at Temnac Bay on Attu Island.   USFWS

Aircraft remains at Fort Glenn on Umnak Island.   COE

Abandoned army barracks at Fort Mears, Dutch Harbor.   COE

Quonset hut and revetment on Adak.

COE

A small Japanese submarine remains at Kiska Harbor.

USFWS

Remains of a coastal artillery gun on Kiska Island. This is possibly the gun captured by the Japanese at Singapore and brought to Kiska in 1942.   USFWS

Japanese anti-aircraft gun facing Kiska Harbor.   USFWS

Abandoned hangar on Amchitka.

Old pier in Constantine Harbor, Amchitka.

Craig Sorenson
Tacoma, Washington

Craig Sorenson
Tacoma, Washington

Three-inch coastal gun on Shemya Island.

COE

A beached Japanese ship at Kiska Harbor.

USFWS

The splinter-proof doorway to an ammunition bunker on one of the islands joined by a man-made causeway from Japonski Island to the westernmost island battery position at entrance to Sitka Sound.

Kermit Edmonds
Missoula, Montana

The interior of an underground bomb and splinter-proof service passageway between battery positions of coastal defense guns on the westernmost island at the entrance to Sitka Sound.

Kermit Edmonds
Missoula, Montana

Japanese machine gun on Kiska Island.

USFWS

Remains of ring-mount assembly for one of three coastal defense battery positions on the
westernmost island guarding entrance to Sitka Island.

Kermit Edmonds
Missoula, Montana

Former Naval Air Station hangars from across Sitka Sound. In the background are the Public Health Service hospital and Mt. Edgecumbe High School.

Old barracks building at Fort Ray. The post was established on Charcoal Island in 1940 and expanded in 1941 to include Alice Island.

photos from
Gary Candelaria   Sitka, Alaska

Runway area now used as a parking lot.

photos from
Gary Candelaria
Sitka, Alaska

Former Bachelor Officers Quarters houses Public Health Service personnel.

Former Alaska Railroad troop sleepers on display at the Alaska Transportation Museum at the State Fairgrounds near Palmer. SC

Shemya Air Force base in 1972. It is now a top-secret defense installation. AAC

BIBLIOGRAPHY

Adelman, Robert and Colonel George Walton, **The Devil's Brigade,** Chilton Books, 1966.

Army, U.S., **The U.S. Army in Alaska,** Pamphlet 360-5, 1976.

Bowman, Phylis, **Muskeg, Rocks and Rain,** Prince Rupert, B.C., 1973.

Driscoll, Joseph, **War Discovers Alaska,** J.B. Lippincott, 1943.

Finnie Richard, **Canol,** Ryder and Ingram, 1945.

Garfield, Brian, **The Thousand Mile War,** Ballantine Books, 1969.

Gilman, William, **Our Hidden Front,** Reynal and Hitchcock, 1944.

Griffin, Harold, **Alaska and the Canadian Northwest,** W. W. Norton, 1944.

Handleman, Howard, **Bridge to Victory,** Random House, 1943.

Jordan, George Racey, **Major Jordan's Diaries,** Harcourt Brace Jovanovich Co., 1952.

Mills, Stephan, **Arctic War Planes, Alaska Aviation of WW II,** Bonanza Books, 1978.

Morgan, Lael, **The Aleutians,** Alaska Northwest Publishing Company, 1980.

Potter, Jean, **Alaska Under Arms,** The Macmillan Co., 1942.

Remley, David, **Crooked Road, The Story of the Alaska Highway,** McGraw Hill Co., 1976.

Slettinius, Edward, **Lend-Lease, Weapon for Victory,** The Macmillan Co., 1944.

Sundborg, George, **Opportunity in Alaska,** The Macmillan Co. 1945.

Thorburn, Lois and Don, **No Tumult, No Shooting, The Story of the PBY,** Henry Holt and Co., 1945.

Wilson, William, **Railroad in the Clouds, The Alaska Railroad in the Age of Steam 1914-1945** Pruett Publishing Co., 1977.

Various articles in **Alaska Magazine, The Alaska Journal, Northern Engineer,** other publications and newspapers and personal remembrances.

APPENDIX

Northwestern Canada comprises 750,000 square miles.   Alaska comprises 586,412 square miles. Operation Landcrab was the invasion of Attu. Operation Cottage was the invasion of Kiska.

From 1940-45, the U.S. Army operated approximately 140 different locations in Alaska as follows: weather stations, railroads, air control and warning service units, support bases, emergency landing fields, Tanana-Yukon River barge service, coast and anti-aircraft artillery batteries, warehouses and terminals, ports, communication systems, infantry garrisons and airfields.

The U.S. Army's principal bases in Alaska were: Adak, Camp Skagway, Excursion Inlet, Forts Glenn, Greely (Kodiak Island), Mears, Randall, Ray, Raymond, Richardson, William H. Seward and Whittier.

The principal U.S. Army Air Force's bases in Alaska were: Adak, Amchitka, Annette Island, Attu, Cape, Elmendorf, Galena, Ladd, Marks, Mile 26, Naknek, Shemya, Station 17, Thornbrough and Yakutat.

The U.S. Navy's principal bases in Alaska were: Atka, Attu, Dutch Harbor, Kodiak, Sitka and Shemya.

Major United States aircraft used in Alaska:

Bell P-39 Aircobra - Designed 1941, very popular with Russian flyers, range 600 to 800 miles.

Bell P-63 Kingcobra - Designed 1942, most were sent to Russia, range 450 miles.

Boeing B-17 Fying Fortress - Designed 1935, over 12,000 built during the war, range 2,000 miles.

Consolidated PBY Catalina - Designed 1935, used in reconnaissance, bombing, antisubmarine warfare, transport and sea rescue. Range 2,350 miles. PBY-5A appeared in 1941 as the first amphibian airplane.

Consolidated B-24 Liberator - Designed 1939, 18,000 built during the war, range 2,000 miles.

Curtiss P-40 Warhawk - Designed 1939, range 700-900 miles. P-40D, used by the Royal Canadian Air Force was called **Kittyhawk.**

Curtis P-36 - Designed 1934, outmoded at the start of the war.

Douglas C-47 Skytrain - Designed 1935, military version of the DC-3, range 1,600 miles, most versatile and common transport plane of the war.

Lockheed P-38 Lightning - Designed 1939, shot down more Japanese planes than any other, range 450 miles.

Lockheed PV-1 Ventura - Designed 1941, land based Navy bomber-reconnaissance plane, range 1,660 miles.

Martin B-26 Marauder - Designed 1939, very difficult plane to fly, range 1,100 miles.

North American B-25 Mitchell - Designed 1940, 900 were shipped to Russia, very versatile bomber, range 1,350 miles.

Major Japanese aircraft used in Alaska:

Kawanishi H6K4 - Designed 1940,, seaplane known as "Mavis", used as a reconnaissance plane and bomber, range 3,780 miles.

Mitsubishi A6M Reisen - Designed 1939, most popular Japanese fighter of the war, known as the "Zero", range 1,900 miles.

Mitsubishi G4M - Designed 1939, most popular Japanese bomber of the war, range 3,700 miles.

Nakajima A6M2-N - Designed 1941, seaplane version of the "Zero", known as "Rufe", range 1,100 miles.

Yokosuka E14Y - Designed 1941, known as "Glen", range 548 miles.

INDEX